THE ROOM OUTSIDE

THE ROOM OUTSIDE

DESIGNING YOUR PERFECT OUTDOOR LIVING SPACE

DAVID STEVENS

PHOTOGRAPHY BY JERRY HARPUR

STERLING

New York / London
www.sterlingpublishing.com

DEDICATION: to all the clients, friends, colleagues and landscapers who have made this book possible

Library of Congress Cataloging-in-Publication Data Available

1 2 3 4 5 6 7 8 9 10

Published in 2007 by Sterling Publishing Co., Inc.
387 Park Avenue South, New York, NY 10016

Text copyright © David Stevens 2007
Photography, design, illustration and layout copyright © 2007 Jacqui Small

Original published in the UK in 2007 by
Jacqui Small, and imprint of Aurum Press Ltd
25 Bedford Avenue, London WC1B 3AT, UK
Distributed in Canada by Sterling Publishing

c/o Canadian Manda Group, 165 Dufferin Street
Toronto, Ontario, Canada M6K 3h6

For information about custom editions, special sales, premium and corporate purchases, please contact Sterling Special Sales Department at 800-805-5489 or specialsales@sterlingpub.com

Manufactured in Singapore

Sterling ISBN-13: 978-1-4027-4866-0

ISBN-10: 1-4027-4866-3

Picture captions

PAGE 1 Inside or out, the same guidelines of space, form, color and detail apply. Some rooms are fully outside, some a halfway house, as here with the raised pool acting as a backdrop to comfortable seating, the cushions picking up the tone of the walls.

PAGE 2 I find much garden seating abominably uncomfortable, so why not set a sofa beneath a shady awning. With modern waterproof fabrics, a shower is no problem and in the event of rain just take the soft elements inside.

ABOVE If you think a house is multifunctional, then a garden can be many times more so, ranging from sitting, dining and entertaining on a whole range of different surfaces, to water in all its guises. Focal points, fountains and furniture are just a few of the elements; choice is only limited by your imagination.

Contents

Introduction

THIS IS NOT A BOOK ABOUT GARDENING or even garden design in the traditional sense, rather an exploration as to how we can use the space around our homes in practical and exciting ways. The whole thrust of gardens has been subtly changing for many years and has now reached a point where the divisions between inside and out are in many cases barely perceptible. Plants move inward, surfaces outward; you will find outside kitchens, bathing places and showers, dining space, playrooms, somewhere to snooze and elegant work areas beyond your backdoors. Dividers and screens, some of them movable, will provide definition; walls are vehicles for water features, mirrors, painting and planting. Music, heating and lighting extend usage at any time of the day, arbors; pergolas and overhead structures cast shade, providing ceilings and privacy.

For my own part I have been designing both interior and exterior space for something like forty years; I know a thing or two about it. It's not a job to me and, however clichéd it may sound, it is simply a way of life, a wonderfully complex and fulfilling way of life that revolves around a subtle blend of the personality of my clients and my own experience. Good designers never force ideas on those they work with, but are facilitators who blend a range of options together.

In reality there is little difference in design terms between inside and out, they are after all both spaces and the rules that guide one, guide the other. Good design, in whatever field, is usually simple and straightforward, although the best also offer subtlety, which takes any composition into the realms of excellence. The one area where rooms outside are different is in the use of plants. These have the ability to quite literally bring a place alive, but it's an interesting, and to me quite

laudable, fact, that much planting is becoming ever more simple. You will see throughout this book that while some gardens and specific rooms are richly planted, just as many rely on the simplest and most straightforward schemes. This is one area where less can certainly be more, particularly where the overall layout is unashamedly architectural. The traditional view that a garden must contain plants is rapidly changing and while they may well serve a purpose, they can also muddy the picture. Add to this the whole question of maintenance and you may find yourself thinking rather differently about that valuable space around your home.

Gardens are for living, gardens are for people and, above all else, gardens are for enjoyment. In *The Room Outside* we bring all these elements together: we manipulate space, we allocate both functional and elegant places and we perceive style. Plants are woven in and around compositions, water divides and defines different areas, color brings vibrancy, linking inside and out.

While we shall look at complete rooms that offer excitement and inspiration we shall also look at features and details, showing you exactly how these can be built or constructed. *The Room Outside* is a refreshingly complete dossier of how to live in your garden, something that more and more of us are doing, with increasing sophistication.

PREVIOUS PAGE This is quite simply a study in the exquisite art of geometry where different materials, planes and elevations combine to produce the ultimate outside room. Here there is ample room to relax on the lower terrace, defined by the crisply trimmed hedge which in turn flanks the slightly elevated walkway set above a rill. Water adds sound and movement while simple planting in raised and ground-level beds softens the underlying architectural lines.

RIGHT You have to be a certain kind of person to enjoy this impeccably detailed composition; I love it. This in many ways is as far from nature as you can get, with each element exquisitely proportioned; yet the trees, surrounding hedges and view to the distant landscape add a natural balance that draws everything together. Success here is brought about by the spatial relationship between the sitting area, lawn and water, offset by the intimacy formed by the overhead canopy.

Living in
the garden

Relaxing

Gardens are for living and to my mind while the various rooms will form a backdrop for all kinds of activities, a key element in all this will be relaxation, which in turn relies on a composition that is tailored around just what you want and the amount of maintenance you are prepared to undertake.

But enjoying a space at your leisure can be more than just sitting or dining: it can encompass play, sport, working out, swimming and many other things for all the family. Add to this somewhere to shower or float in a spa bath when the day is done and you have something pretty close to heaven.

For much of this privacy will be important and here the division of the area with carefully positioned dividers of adequate height will not only provide this, but will give the garden that essential feeling of mystery and surprise as you move from place to place. Overheads and arbors add seclusion and also offer the element of shade to enhance contemplation.

Many people have a far too narrow idea of what a garden is for and in reality you can do things in an outside room that would be difficult inside the house. I have an artist friend who just loves walls, not just for their screening capabilities but as great exterior canvases that she can continually repattern and paint. This metamorphosis not only offers her creative experimentation but has the ability to completely change the look and feel of the entire garden. Other people hang pictures, or simply frames that can outline a feature or object. Never forget the all-important element of humor; it has the ability to bring life and joy into any environment.

Steps, raised beds and slopes are more than just that—they will often offer a place to sit, as well as all kinds of imaginative children's play, usually made up on the spot. Swings can hang from trees, while a broad seat around a stout trunk will double as a table or another play surface.

While the rooms inside your home have all sorts of uses, their counterparts outside offer far more potential and have the advantage of sun, shade, views and just good fresh air. Enjoy them for what they are and relax just as much as you want—after all, it's good for you!

RIGHT The success, or otherwise, of many an outside room lies in the direct linkage with the house or building it adjoins. If the latter can be projected into the landscape there is a natural synergy and this is something an overhanging or cantilevered roof achieves naturally. Broad steps and simple paving extend the bond further, both giving way to the softness of the lawn beyond.

Planning your space

Everybody will use their outdoor space differently, because of personality
and specific requirements. Just how we allocate space is a balance between
the size of the garden and the area needed for a given activity. This will
suggest the dimensions of a room and how it relates to those around it.

One of the real differences between inside and out is the fact that the
house, unless you are lucky enough to plan it from scratch, already has the
room sizes predetermined, but outside it's entirely up to you. Many people
have difficulty in visualizing how big a given area will be. Although you can
draw a plan to scale and work on that, it may be easier to simply go out
into the garden and mark the various areas out with string or a trail of sand.
If you are going to use trellis or fence panels for dividers, then why not get
these first, even before you plan your layout, so that you can experiment
with positioning them in different locations. This really is an excellent way of
visualizing space in a three-dimensional way. They can be simply propped
up and moved about at will until you feel things are just right.

ABOVE Vernacular design, in whatever
field, always embraces a rightness of purpose.
An old store with Roman tiles and local stone
offers the perfect place for an outside sitting
room, sheltered and warmed by an open fire.
How pleasant to sit here on a cool evening,
toasting your toes and sipping the local wine.

RIGHT Relaxation takes many forms, the
ultimate of which is sleeping. But to sleep
outside, on a balmy night, or even in the warmth
of the afternoon is something special indeed.
When the bedroom is open to the fresh air and
nestled beneath the canopy of sturdy trees,
set about with planting you might think
yourself in Eden, although insect repellent
might just be more than a passing fancy.

As far as the actual allocation of space is concerned, it pays to be as realistic as you can about this right from the start. It is also important to bear in mind that any garden, however large or small, has to accommodate the practical and sometimes downright ugly things as well as aesthetically pleasing ones. In order to be able to truly relax, with nothing to jar your enjoyment of the garden, you have to provide a balance between utility and decoration. Of course there are many ways to enhance the former and one of the real ways is to bring the practical element right into the picture. A shed need not be boring, but a rainbow of colors, with trunks or trash cans that can used for storage, integral with the building and having a top that could be planted as a raised bed, and so on.

When you are sitting outside there is a certain amount of psychology at play and it's a fact that if you are open to the wider garden, with nothing around you, you tend to feel vulnerable. On the other hand, a high wall or screen is too claustrophobic. What can be just right is a combination of raised beds, about 18 in. (45 cm) high when so they can double as an occasional seat, perhaps with a built-in barbecue and low planting. If the latter is fragrant then so much the better. All this will still allow you a view out of the area, giving a feeling of space, but it will also provide that necessary feeling of security. In addition it can be worked to form an exit into the room beyond, thus providing a natural progression of space.

Most of us work during the day and much of our leisure time, during the week at least, is spent in the evenings, when things start to cool off. I resisted outdoor heaters for ages, but boy, am I now a convert. They can be gas or electric, free standing or hung from a wall or overhead beams. The only problem is that you tend to stay outside forever and, if you are so inclined, you can seriously deplete the stocks of alcohol!

ABOVE LEFT Nothing fancy here, lots of cushions, mismatched furniture and a simple gravel floor: what more do you want?

LEFT Small can most certainly be beautiful and here a lack of space has been turned to advantage with built-in furniture, a simple lightweight deck and raised beds that shelter this roof room, which is perched above city streets, from the windows opposite.

ABOVE Strong color works well in bright light countries, allowing the cushions and squabs to be the perfect and comfortable counterpoint to the massing of integrated seats and table. The stone wall offers enclosure and the mellow old brick floor a feeling of permanence.

▶ FOLLOWING PAGES Some compositions just appear to float and this delicately worked living room with its subtle cantilevers, attention to detail and raised plinths give it elegant poise.

Hidden corners

Privacy, real privacy, is a joy in gardens of whatever size, large or compact. This means a secret place within the other rooms, a snug or parlor, call it what you will. The great Italian gardens, for all their splendor, always had one of these secluded areas where the family could get away from the sheer scale on display elsewhere. In a tiny garden it could just be a single seat or bench tucked behind a wing of hedge or planting, in a larger space an arbor with overhead beams, set about with fragrant climbers, could shelter table and chairs. Half the enjoyment is just getting there through all the other places with their different moods. On a grander scale there is always a tree house, which if it is big enough can have its own rooms. For total seclusion pull up the ladder and wait till they find you.

BELOW An old bench and color-themed planting make this a delightful place to while away a good deal of time. The paving is practical and the pots a movable feast that can quickly and easily change the look of the place.

RIGHT There is an airy lightness about this intimate and trellised corner that is simply delightful. This is one person's space, eclectic and charming, wrapped about with plants but at the same time offering glimpses to the garden beyond, a room within a room.

ABOVE LEFT This little house is truly a gazebo, a room with a view, nestled as it is within beds of hardy perennials and backed by trees. It would be a good place to sit and write, or perhaps sit and rest to momentarily ease the aching limbs of the gardener.

ABOVE RIGHT Short of room inside—well, move on out. Office, bedroom, playroom or just somewhere to get away, a garden building can offer them all. See how the deck boards turned across the space tend to slow the eye down; run the other way, away from you, they would have accelerated the view.

OPPOSITE There is always a fascination about structures jutting out over water; it's the mingling of elements that's so exciting. There is ample room to relax here surrounded by the view and ever-changing reflections.

Summerhouses

Summerhouses, at least in cooler climates, are pretty much as the name suggests, good for the warmer months. Like arbors they can be a place where you can retreat and as they have a roof are naturally waterproof. Site them carefully—they will be a dominant focal point and really need to be settled in among ample planting. A variation is a gazebo, which in historic terms was always sited to embrace a view, hence "gaze-bo." They should be solid and well built, certainly not those awful wire contraptions sold as such.

Few gardens are large enough for a lake, but some are and they are the most stunning garden feature to be revealed at the turn of a woodland path or at the end of a vista. A boathouse, together with deck and of course a row boat, can be simply gorgeous and can double as mooring, a place for storage, sitting area and play space. Set about with heavy planting of a sufficient scale they are straight out of *Swallows and Amazons* and will be enjoyed by young and old alike, but do have a life-saver handy.

ULTRA SMART URBAN LIVING

If you really want to chill out in the most elegant garden imaginable then this is for you—"cool chic" it most certainly is. From the raised dining area to the precision of the clipped trees on the lower level this is controlled and beautifully executed exterior design at its very best.

But this duo of garden rooms is far more than a designer's whim. There is real style here and every detail has been thought through, not just in and of itself, but in how the spatial relationships and individual components interplay with one another to form a harmonious whole.

You can enter the garden from below or above, something that is not uncommon in an urban situation with access points on varying levels to houses. But this aspect is fascinating nevertheless as it sets up all kinds of possibilities and unusual sight lines across the space

The upper deck offers space for sitting and dining, the two areas being defined by the panelled sections of glass floor, subtly lit from below. To one side a sofa is precisely aligned with two cubes that act as occasional tables while to the other a simple table and four chairs would be just right for a leisurely meal. Carefully positioned blue parasols add strong color and offer shade on a hot day while the deck boards, laid across the space, tend

ELEGANT ENTERTAINING

Sitting, dining and entertaining is the raison d'être of this immaculately detailed garden that seamlessly sweeps from the upper terrace to the clipped formality of trees and lawn below. Nothing is left to chance here, but it is not a composition for the faint-hearted; you have to know your own mind to live here, but if you do then it's perfect.

to visually stabilize the area, gently anchoring it to the width of the house.

Planting here is crisp and minimal, with foliage rather than flowers setting the tone. The clipped box balls in their elegant tapering containers provide an evergreen counterpoint and a striking rhythm that is repeated throughout the space.

From here, beautifully illuminated steps flanked with smooth white walls swoop down to the lower ground floor level, their line offering the only curve in an otherwise completely rectilinear garden. Here a broad paved terrace leads out from the generous doors to the back of the house, the containers of clipped box echoing those set on the terrace above and helping to provide continuity between the two areas. Broad steps lead up to the main garden room, giving way to a perfectly proportioned lawn that has as its focus a well-chosen piece of statuary.

This whole lower garden area is a fascinating counterpoint of planting, entirely in green, used in different ways and at different elevations. At the highest level we have the precisely clipped trees, each having a slightly different character, the overall effect of which is an aerial hedge. This is not pleaching in the strict definition of the word as the branches are not entwined and each individual tree stands sculpturally alone. What they do achieve of course is a perfect screen from the upstairs windows of surrounding houses, an artful solution to an issue that is always a consideration in densely populated urban areas. Instead of there being plants beneath the trees, which would be the normal approach, they rise cleanly from the broad path that encloses the area. Box hedges of different heights and widths add further precise definition.

Using exact geometry in terms of exterior design is extremely demanding and unforgiving, and a common problem is when you are faced with a plot that is at odds with the precise pattern you have created. Here you will see that the bottom boundary is set at an angle to the others and, if you are not careful, this type of abberation will throw all that careful planning out of line. Here, however, the main focal point has been recessed into the solidity of a hedge, the front of which is square with the overall pattern, but the rear conforms to the line of the boundary, a clever solution as this brings all the main components into line.

You could argue that this is a strictly formal composition in that the lower area is mirrored from one side to the other, and you would be right. The refreshing thing is that this kind of modern design thinking has taken the traditional parameters and interpreted them in an entirely fresh and contemporary way, something that is long overdue and one that combines an especially dynamic blend of horticulture, art and architecture—long may it continue.

PERFECT FINISH

This is sophisticated precision taken to its limit. The sofa acts as a divider from the dining area and faces the perfectly aligned cubes with their equally perfect pots. Not sure this would ever work out in our family, but it's a nice touch. Dining on a warm evening with under floor lighting and the solidity of those magnificent pots around you would be easy going indeed; you just need to choose the music! The steps provide the only curving pattern in the composition as they sweep you down to the lower ground floor and garden, the pattern of which unfolds as you draw closer.

THE GARDEN PLAN

Precision and attention to detail is central to this celebration of formal contemporary garden art, from the crisp decking and under-floor lighting of the upper terrace to the manicured hedges and trees that contain the lawn and offer privacy from surrounding properties.

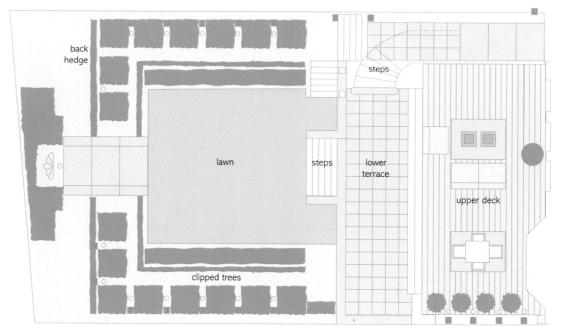

back hedge

steps

lawn

steps

lower terrace

upper deck

clipped trees

Dining

One of the great joys of a garden is being able to cook and eat outside, whether this be with the most simple barbecue or a full-on contemporary kitchen, complete with breakfast bar and dining area. Of course, depending just where you are in the world, weather will play an important role, not just in terms of rain but also protection from a hot sun, without which you simply cannot stay in the garden for long periods of the day.

In inclement conditions a covered and waterproof area can make a deal of sense and you only have to dine in those pavement restaurants, with their roll-down see-through screens, to see just how effective the protection they offer can be, not just from rain, but wind too. In fact it is the latter in temperate climates that prevents many of us from using the garden, so check out the prevailing wind and take account of it.

Something else that is important for a dining area is the psychology of seclusion. To eat in a wide-open situation may be great for a view, but you feel distinctly vulnerable and in turn rather uncomfortable. Rather better to have a degree of fragrant planting both around and above you with partial views to the rooms beyond. Herbs of course are an essential element for an outdoor kitchen and many are handsome as well as practical. Furniture is so often overlooked and above all it should be comfortable—a meal can last for hours, after all. Wherever you are steer clear of white—the glare off a table can be a real problem. Natural colors are far the best and there is little wrong with wood, in all its guises.

The dining area, which will be logically positioned adjoining the house, with easy access from the living room and preferably also the kitchen, really needs a minimum of 13 ft. by 13 ft. (4 m by 4 m) and preferably more if space will allow. Dining rooms outside need to be rather more generous than their counterparts inside: as a general rule take the size of the dining room inside your home and double it. Remember that you need room for a table, chairs and space to move around easily: there is nothing worse than a chair tipping into adjoining plants, complete with you and your drink!

RIGHT This is an extremely inviting spot for pre-dinner drinks, surrounded as it is with lush planting of almost tropical exuberance. Metal and wirework chairs will always need to be given the added layer of comfort that a cushion pad affords if you are going to spending any length of time sitting on them.

Dining at night

Dinner, in our household at least, is the most important meal of the day. It's a time to unwind, chat and more often than not enjoy a beer or three.

Eating outside on a warm evening that gradually moves into dusk and then night is a joy—food seems to taste better, last longer and the whole event is an altogether more laid-back business than if conducted in the house. Lighting is, of course, essential as darkness gathers, and this can be both practical, in guiding you safely to and from the kitchen and other internal rooms, as well as moody, highlighting features and plants and the table itself. On average it's dark for half the year, so make the most of it!

BELOW Dining at night is magical and good lighting essential, the style of which should be respected throughout the garden. This area is sensibly enclosed with built-in seating, the raised planters cleverly softening their outline and linking with the wider composition.

RIGHT To feel comfortable dining outside you really need a feeling of enclosure, with perhaps a glimpse of the wider garden to tempt you before and after the meal. The screen walls are undemandingly simple, the soft terracotta washed with light just softening the line.

Shaded areas

LEFT So often the simple approach works best with practical trestles, a barbecue and planting that presses in on you like a breaking wave. Shade is often a necessity when eating outside and the translucent awning provides this without being overpowering. In order to soften the long wall a humorous abstract provides a splash of color.

BELOW A simple and practical, not to mention sophisticated, dining area is covered by a triangular awning that picks up on the cushions below. This is an intimate space for a good gathering who can get up close if needs be, enclosed by the low walls that echo the stone used in the terrace of the house and giving out onto a broad lawn.

The movement of the sun

A major difference between dining inside and out is the effect of direct sunlight, which of course swings across any area throughout the day. If you have room around the house it can often be attractive and sensible to have a number of places to sit and dine that can chase sun, or shade in a hot climate, as you move through the day. The size of these can reflect the use to which they are put; a breakfast terrace for just a few people will be sensibly smaller and more intimate than somewhere for lunch or dinner that might cater well for friends and relatives. Remember too that the morning and evening will be cooler than midday, when it may be essential to have shelter from a hot sun with a canopy or overheads. I always feel that evening dining rooms are best when open to the sky as you can watch the changing light. Don't switch on the artificial variety too soon; it's amazing how eyesight adjusts and you will naturally see all kinds of wild life that would be impossible in bright or even relatively subtle illumination.

BELOW Where space is limited or the ground slopes steeply then there is no reason why you should not dine on several levels linked by broad steps. The shade from the surrounding mature trees will creep gradually across the lawn and eventually reach the dining table.

OPPOSITE Hot climates need shade; the light is steely with correspondingly deep shadows. Using a massive overhead and natural colors that absorb rather than reflect light creates a wonderful feeling of stability—the perfect outdoor dining room.

Cooking outdoors

Nearly anyone can cook outdoors, the question is how well. The old adage that a workman is only as good as his tools is nonsense—I've tasted great meals (albeit tinged with the slight warmth of a good glass of wine) cooked on the most primitive barbecues. The latter are of course at the simple end of culinary machinery, but there is no doubt that a good, well-made barbecue can produce fine meals, and not just meaty ones. My daughter is a chef and regularly serves us up the most wonderful barbecued fish, vegetable kebabs and other produce straight from the garden, which is my responsibility. To my mind gas barbecues aren't quite as good as charcoal or logs, but that's a personal preference, and many would disagree.

At the other end of the scale, an outside kitchen can be just as good and have just the same equipment as its interior counterpart. Think about the design of the whole area and the relationship of cooker to dining space, worktops and storage—all will be important. Another thing to remember here is the provision of services: water and electricity are essential. These should be thought about before you lay paving or other surfaces and if in any doubt about wiring always consult a professional.

ABOVE Monumental comes to mind, but in such a setting, with the hot sun and the scale of the landscape around, you need to be expansive if an area is not to be dwarfed by its surroundings. Walls and overhead beams give partial enclosure, shade and a frame to the views, while the crisply detailed cast concrete paving offers room to dine close to the built-in barbecue.

ABOVE CENTER In any kitchen generous workspace is essential, which is often the problem with a simple barbecue. There is a satisfying solidity in this layout, and not much distance between cooking and eating areas.

ABOVE RIGHT This is a clever idea, elegant too, with the work surface extending out to form a nearby table which is in turn surrounded by a sitting area of ample size. This is high-tech cooking with carefully positioned lights and easy to clean stainless steel, just the sort of thing any chef would like to get their hands on.

Constructing a brick barbecue and built-in seat

Built-in features save space but you need to think about positioning them to the best advantage—close to a kitchen is ideal for a barbecue. Methods of construction are legion, but brick is flexible, durable and can be used in nearly any configuration. Here a glazed brick worktop is set over a concrete slab that in turn forms the roof of a useful storage cabinet. The barbecue itself can be adjusted for height on built-in steel runners, the bottom of which holds the charcoal tray. A wooden seat can easily be fitted into the angle of a wall and could additionally have a hinged top for further storage.

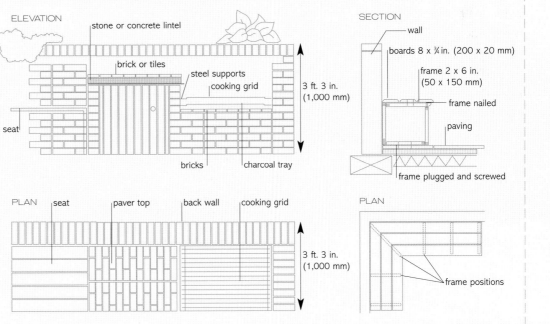

ELEVATION
stone or concrete lintel
brick or tiles
steel supports
cooking grid
seat
3 ft. 3 in. (1,000 mm)
bricks
charcoal tray

PLAN
seat
paver top
back wall
cooking grid
3 ft. 3 in. (1,000 mm)

SECTION
wall
boards 8 x ¾ in. (200 x 20 mm)
frame 2 x 6 in. (50 x 150 mm)
frame nailed
paving
frame plugged and screwed

PLAN
frame positions

THE OUTDOOR CHEF

Depending on where we live in the world and the temperatures and weather conditions we have to contend with, we are more or less tempted to cook in the garden. Let's face it, nothing tastes better than food prepared and eaten outside, whether it be at midday with a canopy of foliage casting dappled shade or as the sun sinks and the air is gently cooling. Alfresco meals are, of course, always eaten outside, but all too often the actual cooking equipment is limited to an undersized barbecue and continual forays to the kitchen to search for tools and other vital equipment, and a great deal of the food preparation takes places indoors.

What fun, what sheer bliss then, to have a fully fledged outdoor kitchen, with a grill, an oven, worktops and all the tools you are likely to need readily to hand. This is truly a chef's paradise, and could be yours too.

But to be realistic such a place needs to be under cover in the more temperate lands and only in the open if the climate is benign enough that inclement winters and rainy days are the exception rather than the rule.

In reality all of this is largely down to a little imagination, and with the advancements in modern technology and the range of materials that are resistant to wet conditions, it is only our inhibitions that really prevent us from cooking and dining in the open far more often.

This is truly a gastronomic garden with space set aside for a purpose-built kitchen that does indeed cater for all the whims of a top-flight chef. A gas hob sits along side a charcoal grill, a deep fryer nestles up with a fridge while pots, pans and other paraphernalia hang within easy reach from stainless steel rails above. Humor is not forgotten

either and beneath the appliances and ample worktop, fish glide and dart in their purpose-built tank, hopefully not to be served up at the next meal. None of this is technically difficult to install: you can use bottled gas or it is quite feasible to have it piped from the house, while electricity is an essential service for many aspects of an outside room, so the supply can be extended to the outdoor kitchen. Do make sure that you use accredited and fully qualified installers, though—you cannot compromise on safety when it comes to these services.

In terms of layout this is also very much a working garden and while not a tiny space it is certainly not large, measuring approximately 49 square feet (15 meters square).

In order to detract from the rectangular boundaries and the static shape the whole design has been turned at a diagonal. This immediately sets up a new dynamic that divides the garden into two main areas. To the right lies the kitchen, the floor of which is a combination of crisp pre-cast concrete paving stones, wood and compacted gravel. This links and gives way to the dining area that is surrounded by a low wall 2 ft. (600 mm) high that both retains the raised bed beyond and also doubles as sitting space—this really comes into its

A COOK'S KITCHEN

Pots of herbs, bananas and other culinary goodies flank and surround this wonderful outdoor kitchen. Fish in a large tank add color and ever-changing patterns while high walls and screens help to shelter the area when it is in use. Even garlic is readily at hand, hanging from the rails above.

own when you have invited a garden full of friends round for a meal, as everyone can find somewhere to perch, with a plate of delicious food in hand.

To the left hand side of the garden the mood changes entirely and here the pattern becomes all the more fluid and relaxing. Gravel and paving gives way to a soft green lawn, stepping stones leading across the area to terminate at a sunken sitting area surrounded by a swooping wall of white rendered concrete blocks with a painted fern adding a clever and delicate touch. This is a secluded place where you can get away from the hustle and bustle of the kitchen for a while, and would also be great for a children's play area, contained as it is by low walls and plans.

The boundary walls are also finished in white render, pierced by oval windows that look into surrounding woodland to "borrow" the views

beyond and coax them into play in the more intimate confines of the composition.

While the garden structure is undoubtedly fun, the planting goes a long way to reinforce this. Species are an eclectic mix of dramatic tree ferns, bananas and fragrant lilies, all standing out in sharp relief against the cool white walls behind. Closer to the kitchen perennials are brought into play, the white heads of agapanthus echoing the clipped box ball, daisies sprawling below while lavender and other herbs are ready for the pot.

At the end of the day this really is a multi-purpose garden; it revels in the unusual but at the same time has the ability to blend seemingly disparate elements together seamlessly. It's not going to be for everyone but I have to say that it would suit me very well, and I guess a good few others down to the ground, and why not!

DIVISION AND DEFINITION

Low walls, the perfect height for sitting and the occasional pot, define the individual rooms, the stone cladding linking with the stepping stones set in gravel. The dining room is just that, with plenty of room to sit comfortably round the table and more space on the walls if necessary. Benches, rather than chairs, are always more cosmopolitan when eating outside, and the whole scene is gently lit in the evening by lighting hidden within the planting.

THE LIVING ROOM

The two halves of the garden
are quite different and this in turn
makes the overall space feel larger,
each room having its own dynamic.
Here the composition is soft and
flowing, a grass carpet and stepping
stones leading to the secret and
sunken garden, wrapped about by
the swooping wall, backed by
planting that in turn is delicately
handled. The subtle painted fern
adds a clever touch, echoing the
species elsewhere in the garden.

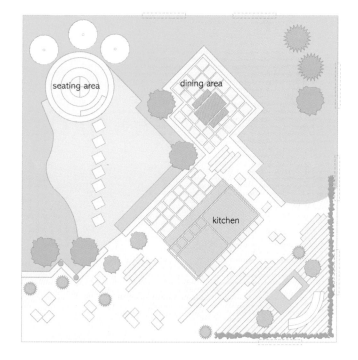

seating area

dining area

kitchen

THE GARDEN PLAN

Diagonal lines used in a
square garden always
engender a feeling of
greater space and in this
situation help define the
cooking and dining areas
and separate them from
the softer lawn and sunken
sitting room. The raised
wooden deck in the
foreground blends neatly
into the gravel and the
other paving set around
the central work area.

THE POND HOUSE

If you wish to dine outside in the utmost contemporary sophistication surrounded by water and other reflective elements, then you could do little better than this extraordinary and wonderfully daring composition.

This is a garden where the designer has been allowed free rein in aesthetic terms, although this is strongly tempered with practicality, an absolute necessity when pools are raised above the level of the adjoining sitting areas, as well as the beautifully detailed building that acts as a pivot to the scheme as a whole.

Although in constructional terms this is not a proejct for the fainthearted, the end result is extraordinarily restful, with still, cool planes of water and mirrors wrapping around you to provide a great feeling of stability and calmness.

It all starts conventionally enough with an old natural stone path leading between softly planted borders, but once up the shallow steps you enter another world as the sharp line of decking leads the eye straight to the extensive glass walls of the garden house. Such glazed surfaces not only give the building an inherent lightness that allows it to float within this extraordinary outside room, but they inevitably make the whole area feel larger; the reflective surfaces of both glass and water offer an ever-changing series of images and

double takes that continually cheat the eye and offer an almost magical feeling of unreality.

But not all is illusion; this is also a carefully planned place of relaxation with room enough for sitting, dining and entertaining. The fact that it is contained within raised pools and planting simply gives a feeling of security and seclusion, once you have mastered the initial fear of flooding. In truth this is not an idle psychological concern as the water laps the edges of the pools and although allowed to cleverly overflow down the reflective sides, it would take a while to accept this as ornament rather than something rather more threatening, particularly as you are sitting well below water level. This same feeling, albeit even more heightened, is apparent when you are actually inside the building—fun though!

And this of course is the point; this is a place of exuberance, of conceptual daring and undoubted

SURROUNDED BY WATER

Control, reflectivity, water, surfaces and the coolest of outside rooms, what a composition! There is a delicate touch here that allows all of these facets to be drawn together in a completely unique yet practical way. This is a garden to live in and enjoy, but is also a place to marvel at.

THE PLANTING

Reflections are remarkable things, adding depth to a view but also allowing one plane to be drawn into another, sometimes without you initially being able to see exactly what is going on. The evergreen planting is an integral part of the composition, doubled by reflectivity, but with a delicate quality that will be enhanced by the slightest breeze.

pleasure, you can only really revel in your surroundings in a situation like this. A touch of playfulness is evident everywhere, from the plumb bobs that dangle tantalizingly close to the water, gently moving in the breeze to the mock mirror that has you looking twice before you are aware that it is really an entrance into the garden.

A great deal of thought has also gone into the materials used for construction and this is largely what gives everything a feeling of stability and continuity. There are really only two, the layered reflective surfaces of glass, steel and water, which in visual terms act as one, and the wood which is used in the decking, the furniture and the surrounding screens. The latter are built from

simple vertical boards that also echo the lines of deck and even the table. See also how the slatted screen set on one corner of the pond is reflected back in the water, increasing its apparent height and adding yet another double take to the overall picture.

But the best part of all has to be the roof; like the walls this is also made from glass, incorporating slate-gray screens as a protection from the sun. So when it rains the water is everywhere, sliding, rolling, dripping and dropping over the edges. Instead of keeping everything close to the ground here we have the element taken up above us, with water all around. The roof surface provides shimmering reflections of clouds and sky, birds, trees and surrounding buildings, all softened and gently distorted into constantly changing patterns.

This really is what creativity is all about. A designer should never impose their own regime but rather be a facilitator, stretching their own imagination if it's all down to them, or taking their clients' ideas, and then adding their own to create a synergy between the two that lifts one set of parameters into an altogether different plane. Good design is about stretching the imagination, not too far, but as far as both parties are prepared to go. There is a delicate line between sensitivity and egotism that can be the making or breaking of any work of art and this garden, above all else, is surely that.

GARDEN PLAN

This is a design of positive and negative space in so much that the solid surfaces hold the composition together while their mirrored counterparts do their best to fragment the underlying geometry. All of this could so easily have become a mess but a firm hand, a keen eye and a vivid imagination are the arbiters of success.

Playing

Children's play can and should happen just anywhere, but it is sensible, if there is room, to provide both hard and soft surfaces. When they are young it's good to be able to keep an eye on them, so an extension of your main sitting area will be ideal, both for wheeled toys and general fun. Sandpits are always popular and can either be set into a paved area with a wooden cover that can be placed over them when not in use, or be the portable variety that can chase shade rather than sun. Paddling is something that is irresistible for youngsters and grown-ups alike on a sunny day and I've built a few good pools, again within a paved area but with a floor of smooth cobbles that give a textured and largely non-slip bottom. There could be a place for a shower set above—children will love this on a hot day and so will the older members of the family. If you are modest, a neatly detailed wooden screen will be just fine. Remember that in this world of decreasing water supplies the run-off could form an ideal supply for the garden.

It's also a fact that as children get older—and as a grandparent I know a bit about this—they like to get away from it all. Secret places, such as a fort surrounded by a bamboo grove, a makeshift shelter from tree prunings or a sheet strung from branches will provide hours of fun. You can't tell children where to play—they will make their own rooms and good luck to them. Just don't give them one of those frightful plastic houses—they look awful and rarely get used. The good old-fashioned den is the place to be!

Tree houses

Think of the possibilities of a tree house, either for children or adults. Safety is of course paramount and a fine set of branches that have been vetted by a tree surgeon are the starting point. For youngsters you will want to utilize something relatively low. A simple platform with a canvas awning is most easily constructed, but walls will add to the feeling of getting away from parents and provide rather more security. Ropes and rope ladders are hopeless for getting up and down and you really need a stout staircase or

RIGHT Not quite a tree house, more like a room on stilts, but great fun nevertheless. With all those potted and climbing plants this one is for the grown-ups, or at least growing-ups, but they should be able to play too! In most gardens there is a time and place for romanticism— it wouldn't be bad up there sharing a bottle of wine and looking out over the garden.

some kind of sloping drawbridge that can be pulled up to deter the enemy. Grown-up tree houses are works of art and there are specialist companies who will build one for you to a selected pattern. Some of these are just fantastic: I've seen wildly gothic Harry Potter or Arthur Rackham-style creations that can sit and dine a dozen people. Fully-fitted kitchens are possible, as well as sleeping quarters. The latter are sometimes essential after a fine meal accompanied by equally fine wine, as a descent to ground level with a breeze blowing is nothing short of hazardous.

Elevated rooms can also be built on stilts, and anyone who has been to a hot climate, Africa in particular, will have seen wonderful buildings constructed in this way. The great advantage of such a place is that it can often be built high enough and orientated to catch a view, something that you will have checked out right at the start of the planning process. You only need to elevate the floor by a few feet to see clear over a hedge or wall, or through a gap between tree canopies. Again you can buy these off the peg and they are often sold or constructed as hides for people to watch birds or other animals, and, come to think of it, they can be used for this in a garden as well as some of the activities just mentioned.

BELOW LEFT Adventures start here: ford the raging torrent and scramble for the cabin before the posse gets you. On the other hand, take a blues guitar and a bottle of moonshine; it's whatever turns you on really, perfect!

BELOW This is a just hatched woven cocoon or egg that could dream up endless possibilities. On a more practical note, such a structure would provide much needed shade on a hot day.

RIGHT The ultimate play space, designed by a grown-up who remembers just what it was like to have real fun. Swing, climbing frame, sturdy ladders to scramble on and a place for storage, fort or a den, as well as a sensible soft lawn to break a fall or for all kinds of games.

BELOW RIGHT A great stockade set inside the moat and well above the grass to get a good view of the approaching army. Once they are within range let loose and then fall back into the castle for the final showdown.

Play equipment

Bigger pieces of play equipment, such as climbing frames, slides and swings or the increasingly popular trampoline, do need to be out in the open, and are usually pretty ugly. A screened self-contained play room is a great idea. As children grow, needs change and the room, by now well protected with hedges or something equally tough, will be perfect for ball games and general mayhem. The very fact that you cannot see what they are doing will score highly in their book. In any garden a wall for kicking or hitting a ball against is invaluable, preferably not near windows! One of your dividers could easily be a wall with lawn or hard surfacing in front—irresistible for budding sports people. Games like tennis take up huge areas and the courts look terrible. If you have the room to spare then screen it and let the children use the all-weather surface for soccer during the winter to keep them off the grass—your lawn will remain in much better condition.

Children's areas

ABOVE At first sight rather scary, this is just fun and a wonderful shower for all kinds of play.

TOP LEFT Kids love color, the more of it the better. They also like slides, platforms, climbing nets and sturdy ladders, all here in abundance. Chipped bark is a sensible low-cost surface, ideal for play and able to absorb the odd fall.

BOTTOM LEFT Wow, this would be good fun! Water is completely irresistible to children and it is sensibly raised here to minimize accidents. Boat or stick races, dams, bobbing balls or just a good splash—great!

OPPOSITE This is a domestic playground on a grand scale, full of pattern and color with a soft rubberized floor. Basketball, climbing on a great fiberglass rock, and ball games of all kinds keep parents and children happy for hours.

Swimming pools

A swimming pool is the ultimate in play equipment that both adults and children can enjoy and benefit from (though children must be supervised in or near water at all times of course), and it requires a great deal of planning in order to incorporate it smoothly into your outdoor room. Depending on where you live in the world, a pool will get more or less use. In a hot climate where they will experience almost year-round use they can, if well designed, sit very comfortably close to a house, and be linked to a relaxing space or dining area. Equally they can occupy their own space, within a walled, screened or secluded area in a separate room of their own, dedicated to their use and hidden from the rest of the garden.

Full-size pools take up a lot of ground but smaller pools, fitted with a jet stream device so that you can swim against the current, effectively swimming on the spot, can fit in a remarkably small space and look good with it. Or you can be creative with the shape and install a long narrow lap pool down one side of a garden. Hot tubs are a close relative to a pool, and if sited well, flush with a terrace or deck, are both elegant and an asset. Beware though of the pseudo-Austrian chalet, complete with sauna and other dubious methods of torture: they look what they are, pretentious.

OPPOSITE Some pools are exceptionally elegant and those with an infinity edge that allows them to merge into the distant landscape are doubly so. The reflections on the still surface offer a huge visual asset.

ABOVE LEFT Circular or kidney shaped pools are more for relaxation than serious swimming and the hammock alongside suggests just that. If you fit an artificial current, however, you can get as much exercise as you want.

ABOVE RIGHT There is always a sense of drama when you enter a pool by broad steps, rather like a Roman bath. This is the ideal shape for a good swim, a simple rectangle that fits neatly within the limited space available.

▶ FOLLOWING PAGES This is cool, very cool indeed, with superb attention to detail both in terms of the surrounding paving and the overhead structure. In contrast to the rectangular pool plan the mosaic serpentine wall brings fluidity to the scheme, and you can finish the day with a gently illuminated barbecue.

HOLLYWOOD INDULGENCE

Dreams can be wonderful things, inspirational and fun, while remaining elusively unattainable and somewhat impractical. But are they so out of reach? Sometimes we see something that although seemingly impossible still has elements within it that we can garner, fashion to our own individual needs and at the end of the day be the basis of something totally achievable that suits us down to the ground.

This is a little piece of Moorish heaven, with overtones of the Alhambra, sheets of water, cool cloisters and a delicate fountain. So what if it is in Hollywood, so what if it seems too good to be true with its background of azure blue skies and bougainvillea-clad walls? There are some good ideas contained within this glamorous garden that we can surely benefit from.

The first of these is simplicity, the basis of all good design and the driver of many a fine composition. This is a generous outside room, but one that is perfectly suited to its main purpose of leisure, pleasure and relaxation. This is a fun place to be and to spend time.

In essence there are three rooms here; the first as you exit the house with ample room to chill out and various comfortable seating groups to choose from; the second for sitting and dining in the shade of an arched cloister; and a third for water play

RELAXING RETREAT

From the sun-drenched loungers at the far end of the pool to the sophisticated elegance of a Moorish courtyard adjoining the house that looks into and through arched dining area to the garden beyond, this is a composition for all moods. Sitting, dining and simply enjoying yourself are all easy.

and swimming. The cloister idea is particularly clever, close enough to the kitchen for easy access and acting as a natural divider between the activity of the pool area and the serenity of the house. Sitting and dining around the long table, with the sound of crickets in the evening and the glow of candles set in the chandelier above would make this a pretty special place to dine. Some chandelier too!

The whole garden is a formal design, with a central axis that runs from the center of the low raised pool at one end, through the dining area and Roman-ended swimming pool to terminate in the middle of the curved wall in the distance.

Let's face it, this is a pretty tasteful design and a great deal of this tastefulness lies in a careful lack of unnecessary ostentation and real attention

to the smaller details, something that should always be paramount in any form of design, inside or out, whatever the style or situation.

In a garden which is very much geared toward enjoying yourself privacy is important, and here the high clean white walls of the house provide just that. The only danger with white, in such a bright light country, is glare, another good reason for keeping the main sitting and dining area in shade. It is interesting that in the Alhambra the walls were either of a warm-colored stone or beautifully decorated in blues, reds and gold, all of which would tend to absorb rather than reflect light. On the other hand, white offers terrific contrast, both in terms of shadow from well-placed plants or structures and the liberal use of strong color in the form of climbing plants in full flower. Here, the architectural planting and abundant scrambling climbers soften the potentially harsh line of the surrounding walls.

There is also the undeniable drama of moving from the extremes of deep shade, into sun, and back again. You can therefore argue that both finishes have their merit; you just need to be aware of the advantages or otherwise of either.

While water in a Moorish garden is largely used for decoration, a swimming pool can offer both this, and a place of huge enjoyment. At one moment it offers pristine reflections of buildings and sky, the next it is turmoil. This pool is eminently practical too, long enough for a good swim and a simple shape, something largely forgotten by many an installer. Swimming in a hot climate is best done in the morning or the evening and what better than to towel off with the smell of cedar wood burning in the fireplace or even better a barbecue cooking to tempt the palette.

In the last analysis this is a garden of indulgence and play, with fun available for all and large spoonfuls of elegance mixed in for good measure.

PRACTICAL ELEGANCE

The swimming pool occupies a good deal of the floor in this courtyard, offering reflections and a cooling influence to the area as a whole. The fireplace is not only a practical working feature but it is beautifully detailed, the chimney neatly slotting between the two wings of wall. In the heat of the day, the table set in the cloister, bathed in shade, is delightful and eminently useable. This is a series of garden rooms with real purpose, and it works.

THE GARDEN PLAN

Formality is ageless and there is always something reassuring about the stability and plain common sense of such a design. There is a satisfying balance between the sitting area positioned close to the house and the pool beyond, linking by the shady dining area.

courtyard

covered dining area

swimming pool

Working

There are an increasing number of contemporary garden buildings on the market that are remarkably handsome. Often these are home offices, but they will double equally well as a place to sit and a place to sensibly store items such as garden furniture through the colder winter months. Such buildings naturally blend well with modern architecture, although if they are set in a more distant garden room an obvious link with a house is not so pertinent. Some are now fully insulated and have double glazing, so if you run power to them heating and lighting is a natural addition, extending their use into the evening and across the seasons.

The purposes to which they are put are numerous: office, spare bedroom, rumpus room, studio, workshop, you name it. Buildings situated away from the main house have their own specific character; they are places to get away, be quiet and do something that is divorced from the hustle and bustle of the main dwelling. To be genuinely successful they need to be self-contained. There is nothing worse than settling down to work, getting involved with the task in hand and then finding yourself having to tramp back in the pouring rain to have a cup of coffee.

The real secret is space, large enough to fulfill the prime function of the building, but also room for a small kitchen, or at the very least cupboards and a kettle. If you can fit a sink that's always going to be handy and I certainly know a few colleagues who have gone so far as to fit a toilet, running it of course to the appropriate drain.

Purpose-built offices and studios can be expensive things to buy, and there are lots of companies offering a specialist service supplying and installing them, but when you really look at them they are often nothing more than a large shed. If you are that way inclined, or have a good carpenter, it can be quite possible to either build something from scratch or indeed purchase a large shed, insulate it effectively, run the services from the house in the correct conduits, with safety in mind and create a personalized workplace that suits you perfectly. In reality it is insulation

RIGHT Gardens can be multifunctional places, able to cater for office or household chores as well as storage, compost and other related horticultural tasks. There is a refreshing unity in this design that establishes the building within the garden in the use of wood on the comfortable terrace and the environmentally conscious and attractive "living" roof.

from cold and particularly damp that is important, so day and night heating will therefore be essential in a damp climate, particularly in winter. Do bear in mind that buildings over a certain size can require consent from your local authority, and much of this has to do with permanence. In other words a toilet or other water supply and associated drainage might place a building in this category, so if in doubt, check before you start work.

In this day and age telephones and computers are essential for an office and while you can certainly use wi-fi to a transmitter in the main house it might well be worth running in a separate dedicated line.

BELOW An office on the water: Decks have the ability to float over the surface and settle themselves gently into the composition.

TOP RIGHT Simplicity in construction and subtlety in positioning make this office a joy to work in. Elevated, it is secluded and attractive.

BOTTOM RIGHT Isn't this delightful? It's a little sentry box of a building, but neat and full of purpose at the same time. It's a focal point, but one that is quiet and unassuming.

Storage

The problem with most of us is that we have too much stuff. Just what that stuff is can range from lawn mowers to golf clubs, kid's bikes to punctured rubber dinghies—you name it we've got it. If you are anything like me it's difficult to throw things away, however well-intentioned we are, and, that being the case, there is in most outdoor rooms a desperate need for storage. The smaller the space the more critical this is, but before you rush out and simply buy a shed, or load everything into a summerhouse that should be used for far better things, just think of other possibilities.

Here again you take a cue from your inside space. Look around you, where do you put things? Well most of us use that valuable space under the stairs and in many a basement there will be steps with a similar void below. Paint it out, fit shelves and doors and you have a place for permanent storage. What else do we do in our homes? Well, cupboards and wardrobes work pretty well inside and can do the same in a yard. I'm not talking fake wood and laminates here that fall to bits after the first shower, but good old pieces, usually in need of some care and attention that you can pick up in a junk shop. Waterproof them, color them, outrageously if you like, and let them become part of an eclectic living space.

Sheds and utility areas

Utility needs to be thought about sensibly and planned accordingly. In a yard, built-in seats can double for storage within, or an old outhouse can become an excellent tool shed. On a larger scale group buildings together: store house, greenhouse, compost bins, incinerator and so on. Give yourself a good hard-surfaced work area around them and link it back into the wider composition with a generous path which will double for kids on speeding bikes. Screen it with what you like—hedge, planting walls, trellis—and why not let this divider act as a backdrop to a sitting area on the other side, perhaps with overhead beams and surrounded by planting?

If you are growing things to eat don't just hide them away. Of course you can have a dedicated area, but how much better, particularly if space is limited, to grow your crops mixed in with more decorative plants. Many vegetables and, of course, herbs, are frankly good looking in their own right and will grow quite happily in herbaceaous flower beds, and runner beans are one of the best annual climbers you can have.

But the truth of the matter is that any of these options might be too small to cope with your needs, and a shed may be the only sensible alternative. In a small garden it may be impossible to screen it, but why should you—better to make it something special. Time was when sheds were all dreary little buildings, and to be fair there are still plenty of these around today, but with imagination and flair something from your local garden center that looks uncompromisingly dull can be transformed into a delightful focal point—it just takes imagination. Paint brushes are the best bet and you can either make a real statement by introducing a rainbow or be slightly more restrained by linking the color to a scheme elsewhere in the room, that of overhead beams or a washed wall. Window glass need not be clear but stained, and why not add a cut-glass doorknob and escutcheon plate, what fun! Remember that sheds have walls and you can both hang things on them and grow plants up them, often increasing the usable vertical space of the garden as a consequence.

ABOVE Sheds are the ugly ducklings of the garden, unloved, tucked away and usually ignored as much as possible. Give them a break, a coat of paint, a little care and attention and even the most mundane little building will sparkle and become a real ream player, particularly in the smallest of spaces.

TOP RIGHT Of course, a bit of style, with a smartly curved lead or zinc roof and a handsome paint scheme improves things even more, the shed is now a focal point rather than an embarrassment.

BOTTOM RIGHT Living roofs are great fun, providing color and interest throughout the year as well as injecting a little humor into a situation. These sprawling sempervivums are just the job, not only bringing the place alive but allowing it to blend into the background.

Planting a sedum roof

To construct a living roof you will need a tough butyl pond liner, pressure-treated boards that will form a framework, and stout posts to hold the frame in position and take the load off the shed or other structure. Concrete the posts in position first, checking for level, and ensure the height is sufficient to accept the framework. Construct the latter from 6 in. (150 mm) deep boards and screw it back into the supporting posts. Fill the sections with lightweight compost and plant up with a selection of sedums or similar drought-resistant species.

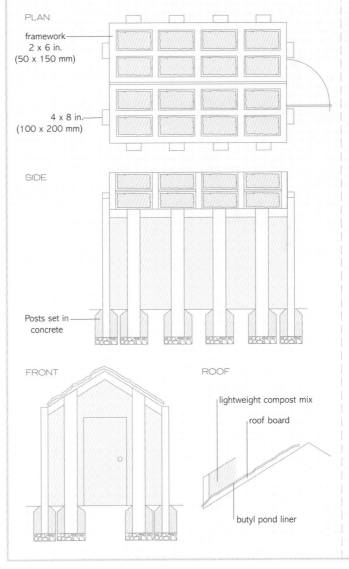

PLAN

framework 2 x 6 in. (50 x 150 mm)

4 x 8 in. (100 x 200 mm)

SIDE

Posts set in concrete

FRONT

ROOF

lightweight compost mix

roof board

butyl pond liner

Designing rooms

Analyzing the plot

Personality, above all else, determines the way we live. Our preference of style, colors, architecture and art, music, literature, favorite places, the car we drive and what we wear—all are motivated by this all-important factor. Some of us are more adept at organizing our living space than others, but everyone, through the magic of personality, is able to put their own stamp on the places in which they live, which is precisely why, thank goodness, no two people or two homes are ever alike.

In terms of a living environment, the most important factor is how we handle space. Great architects, truly great architects, of whom there have been very few, have an innate understanding of space, materials and the qualities of a given site. Frank Lloyd Wright, the master of "organic" architecture and space, produced the most extraordinary buildings, many of which are well over one hundred years old with the ability to still enthrall us today. A favorite Wright trick was not to have a conventional front door, slap in the middle of the house, but to take you round the side, which naturally offers a feeling of mystery. Once through the door the hall could be high or low depending on the mood of the building, and then you are taken on a journey through the place: surprises here, drama there, different volumes, wide, narrow, up stairs, down steps, large rooms, smaller rooms, focal points, views and, of course, the often imperceptible linkage between inside and out. Now we are not all so talented, nor do we have to be, but as soon as we start to grasp just how we can manipulate space and just what it can do for us, we have the essential tools for living outside.

If you look at a house being built, the foundation often looks tiny—how on earth could anyone inhabit such a small area? As soon, however, as the walls start to go up, the doorways are formed and the rooms defined then the whole perspective changes. Yes, this is a house; we can see a kitchen, dining room, hallway and lounge. There is a way through, each place links with the next and each space has its own purpose and theme, you can live in it! So, too, do these principles apply in the garden.

RIGHT Many people would be put off on first seeing such a small unpromising, undeveloped space, but given imagination and a helping of flair this has been transformed into the perfect outside room. In essence there is nothing difficult here: simple white walls that pick up the tone from inside, built-in furniture, a small pool and carefully clipped planting that just adds a touch of softness to the overall picture.

LEFT The division of space is the making of many a successful garden and there are two methods employed here, firstly the broad pool that slows you down as you circumnavigate it and then the two wings of hedge. These naturally focus and draw attention to the white seat set within a clipped arch and made all the more telling by the dark background.

BELOW LEFT That gardens are art is an old adage and this abstract roof garden illustrates the point perfectly. The stainless steel irregularly raised beds are planted with drought-tolerant species, echoed by the containers, while the translucent screen offers shelter and privacy. The floor, a low-maintenance combination of loose cobbles, lightweight paving and decking, acts as a frame to the central "picture."

BELOW RIGHT Not all dividers by any means are hedges: Screens in a whole range of materials, overhead structures, seats, benches and even different surfaces will delineate a space and make the journey through it all the more exciting. The lack of plants here simply maximizes the area for play, sitting and anything else that comes to mind.

Planning the space

A garden with no divisions, like the bare foundation of a house, is all too obvious. Everything is seen at a glance without any of the fascination of knowing just what lies behind a screen or divider, wall or hedge. Views that are glimpsed outside the boundaries are also important and are very much a part of how you shape your rooms. So too is shelter, as a wide-open vista may bring with it the disadvantage of a howling wind! This is of course the great difference between living inside and outside, the latter has weather, of all kinds, which needs to be taken into account.

When you are moving into a new home you would never think of buying a carpet without checking the size of a room or planning a kitchen or bathroom unless you have the exact measurements. Smooth plaster inside the house may be just right for a contemporary painting while exposed stone or brickwork the perfect foil for a tapestry. It's just the same outside—you simply cannot plan your rooms here without checking all the details. While this will naturally include measurements you should also check just what the boundaries are made from, and if there are any changes in level, which may in itself define a particular space. Look at existing floor coverings in terms of paving, grass or other surfaces and, of course, make a note of the position of trees and plants. While a room in your house with a particular

aspect may be sunny or less well-lit, the same principle applies outside: check just where the sun swings throughout the day and in addition see if there is a prevailing wind that blows from a particular direction.

All of this will suggest just how you create and use these spaces and here too is where a degree of common sense is essential. A kitchen inside will often suggest a similar use just outside—a barbecue with an ample paved area, perhaps with beams over to screen a neighbor's window and provide dappled shade. There might be room here to sit and dine, as well as for children to play on a flat dry surface. A raised pool, or beds, built-in seating, storage for toys, and somewhere for the trashcan: all are possibilities. Fragrant planting may provide a sense of enclosure, or a trellis screen and archway,

FAR LEFT Much of the success of outdoor rooms is due to their linkage with those inside. There is a great feeling of continuity here, with the white birch echoing columns and the cubes of box picking up the style of architecture.

LEFT There is nothing fancy here, simply good clean design. The deck offers ample room for sitting and dining while planting acts as a low-maintenance frame and offers privacy.

ABOVE This is one of my favorite gardens: great tumbled and colored slabs of concrete, leaning trees and simple groundcover. It's also the perfect living room, with more than enough room to sit and dine, again with minimum disruption between inside and out.

with their ability to be glimpsed through, provide the division for more boisterous play beyond. This in turn might lead to a secret seat and finally to a utility room, as useful and necessary in the garden as it is indoors.

In a tiny yard all the surfaces may be paved, but you can still create a sense of moving from one place to another, over a pool, behind a wing wall, up a couple of steps. In such small spaces, though, the walls or boundaries may come into their own, as they often have more area and potential than the floors. Niches can be set in stonework or carved from a hedge, a "moon gate" formed in a trellis to focus on a fine planter, while mirrors and murals and other decoration create yet another dimension. Tables can hinge down from a wall or sunloungers pivot up from a deck. Clever lighting will extend use and highlight features while a hammock, that most comfortable sleeping place, will pack away to nothing when not in use.

A LONG NARROW PLOT

When you really look sensitively at a plot before it is designed or developed, a number of ideas and thoughts pass through your mind, some of which perhaps relate to the existing features, the surroundings, any borrowed landscape, and of course your own preferences as to what you want from a garden. This is an essential part of that vital information gathering that sets the parameters of the finished garden to come, and if carried out with a combination of practicality and sensitivity will guide you towards a composition that is both right for you and reflects the character of the immediate area.

This garden, which really is a series of outside rooms, is a real favorite of mine, but that could be because I designed it! Not all compositions that one creates are necessarily so, but here everything came together in terms of the clients I was working with and just what they wanted to achieve, the character of the original site and, equally importantly, the quality of the contractor, who built everything specified to perfection.

We have already looked in detail as to the whole question of how important it is that your personality comes though in a garden in order that you are able to feel comfortable in it and enjoy spending time there, and here I took a delight in interpreting this design mandate in the most positive way possible.

The architecture that sets the theme for this area is classic, set in a Georgian city with its roots going back to Roman times. The prevailing material is stone, the house, surrounding walls and much of the existing paving being built from it. The site is long and narrow, a common shape and size for a town garden, and the views, although made up mostly of the surrounding properties, is good in so much that the buildings are visually all of a piece, bringing stability and cohesion to the surroundings, with nothing untoward on the horizon to jar the sensitivities.

INTERLOCKING INTEREST

Room to sit and dine, a Roman cobble mosaic and a trellis moon gate which echoes the shape of the latter all contribute to bring interest to this long narrow garden. Changes in level have been subtly handled with broad, generous steps which turn across the garden to visually widen the space.

Some people just want a garden in which to relax, entertain, and pursue a hobby, and there is nothing wrong in doing that, but my clients wanted rather more than that, in so much that they wished to introduce and reflect the Roman history of the location. They didn't want a set piece that would dominate the garden, but rather some subtle overtones of what had been before.

But before looking at detail, the bones of any scheme have to be laid down and a long narrow garden is perfect for subdivision, each room or area having its own purpose or theme.

Moving away from the house I have provided ample room for sitting and dining, the prevailing material being a high-quality precast concrete paving that picks up the same color as the garden walls and adjoining architecture. As a secondary surface, that frames the area and acts as bands running through the entire garden, I have introduced terracotta tiles. The repeated lines of these, running from side boundary to side boundary, help to visually widen the space and also hark back into history, as the Romans had a fondness for the same material. As a pivot to the sitting area I designed a mosaic, again a Roman favorite, but in order for tables and chairs to be set on a stable surface that would not cause any upsets this had to be impeccably laid.

This first room is contained by both a broad pool, with a simple Roman waterspout feeding into it, and trellis, the wings of which overlap to allow the steps beyond to be hidden, allowing the journey through the space to be all the more intriguing. Within the trellis is an open circular

ADDING TEXTURE

With an architectural design sensitive planting is essential to soften the underlying outline and provide color and interest across the seasons. This is a garden where divisions drive the composition, the long pool and wings of trellis taking you on a journey from one side to the other and finally to a focal point at the top of the garden.

cut-out which acts as a frame for the view and allows you to focus on a seat at the top of the garden. But this is a glimpse only—you have to walk through the whole of the garden to get there and this is what makes the journey interesting. As you climb the steps behind the trellis your view is temporarily held by a fine urn, from here you turn again, climbing a final step to the small sitting area set at the top end of the garden.

Even in a small garden the utility items are still essential and a garden shed and work area is neatly screened so as to be intrusive—remember, any successful composition has to cater for the mundane as well as the beautiful.

Planting finally softens the architectural outline of the spaces, reinforcing the pattern but at the same time bringing color and interest across the seasons with form, texture and, as a final nod to the Romans, a drift of acanthus, the leaf of which is the motif at the top of Corinthian columns.

THE GARDEN PLAN

Proportion, space and movement are nowhere more apparent than in this series of outside rooms. Materials have been chosen with care and the areas of planting are perfectly balanced to add interest and counterpoint. Add to this the feeling of tension, mystery and surprise and all the classic garden design elements are here.

Garden styles

There is a lot of nonsense talked about garden style, a great deal of it put about by the media who simply want to sell a magazine or garden show. Style, in reality, is what suits you, it's what you feel comfortable with and it's what you can live with over as long a period as you want. Fashion is often blamed, quite wrongly, for poor design and while much of it can indeed be frothy, it can also be both fun and worthwhile. Why on earth should our rooms outside stay the same forever, locked in some kind of horticultural time warp simply because this is so often the traditional concept of a garden? Personally I love fiddling with things and I do it at home all the time by changing the color of walls, moving furniture and focal points around, resiting screens, plants and anything else that takes my fancy. This is something that everyone frequently does inside their homes, or they should, so why should it be any different outside?

I go into many homes—it's one of the privileges of being a designer— and you can tell an awful lot about character by just looking around you. Personally I'm alarmed by places that are simply too tidy, with nothing out of place and not a speck of dust in sight. A comfortable living space is just that, like a well-worn glove or comfortable pair of walking shoes. The problem can be that people kid themselves into thinking that they are someone that they are not—it's those wretched makeover shows and glossy magazines again! These houses seem false, they lack any sense of identity and character, they are quite simply boring. If you create anything then do it honestly and forget what other people think; it's your place, both inside and out, to do with what you will.

On the whole we tend to live in an area we like and we choose a house for the same reason; we have an affinity for it. Whether it is comfortably traditional or unashamedly modern is down to us, which is exactly as it should be. How you furnish it will follow suit: it would be unusual, although not impossible, to fill a fine old country cottage with stainless steel and glass furniture. In other words the style of building and its period will suggest,

RIGHT Now this is a garden with a definite sense of personality. There are some bold choices, from the characterful *Xanthorrhoea* to the screen adjoining the pergola that looks like a piece of modern art with its moon gate and geometric detailing. Planting is kept suitably architectural to complement the crisp and perfectly rendered hard landscaping.

usually quite unconsciously, how we treat it and fill it. Of course you can buck the trend and be simply outrageous, nothing wrong with that, and if handled with panache it can be stunningly successful, but you do need to know what you are doing for it not to look simply pretentious! All I am saying here is to be aware of who you really are and what you like; if you do that then everything should follow on as matter of course.

There should be no real separation between interior and exterior space: The rooms, wherever they are, should just flow naturally from one to another. But rooms situated outdoors also embrace what lies beyond them, in terms of both good views, which, in the hands of a skillful designer, can be drawn into a composition, or something less attractive, which might need to be screened. In other words there can be no distinction in your living space between inside, outside and what lies beyond; they all intermingle and are all equally important players in the overall organization of our rooms outside. This is something we call "borrowed landscape" and it can have an enormous influence in making an area feel larger than it really is.

LEFT Formality can be traditional or contemporary and both can be stunningly successful with the right degree of flair. This is an immensely stable composition with the low rectangles of hedge defining the lawn and the taller trees controlling upper space and providing a screen.

BELOW LEFT Simple and straightforward, with warm color-washed walls that form an easy backdrop to this outside dining room. Nothing ostentatious here, just room to enjoy yourself and push the chairs back after a good meal. It's true the simple things often work best.

BELOW A formal rill leading to a charmingly pretty ironwork bench has been given a sense of movement and airiness with the series of small water jets and loose planting of pale blue irises.

Formal style

In reality there are only two styles of exterior design: formal and informal. Forget about cottage garden style, freeform, Japanese, Italianate, Californian and so on, or whatever is the current favorite, all or any of these can be either formal or informal and both can suitable in a wide range of situations.

Formality simply means producing a regular pattern so that one part of a design or area mirrors another. It can be simple or complex, occupy the whole of a garden or be repeated throughout any number of different sub-divisions. The whole thrust of formality relies on balance, equally about a fulcrum, which in terms of design means a dividing line down or across a space. A formal style sits comfortably with classical or traditional houses where the exterior is balanced, perhaps with a central doorway and a similar number of windows to either side. In this case you might think of a sitting area or terrace that extends equally either side of a central axis, which in turn would lead from the center of the building and pass exactly through the middle of steps that perhaps climb to a higher level. Here might be a pattern

ABOVE Not all gardens are high-tech, some are just comfortable places that suit their owners down to the ground. There is plenty of room here for all kinds of activity with planting both softening and providing privacy to the composition as a whole.

OPPOSITE Rills are the very stuff of a formal layout and this centralized canal, terminating in the pool, offers a delicate counterpoint to the mirrored planting to either side. This in turn focuses on the statue at the end of the vista which acts as a positive full stop.

or parterre of hedging, which might take its cue from half timbering on the house, again one side balancing the other and given over to planting or herbs. Halfway down this room there might be a cross axis, at right angles to the first and defined by a pergola. To either side could be two more spaces with seats, looking toward one another, while in the middle, where the axes cross, a pool. At the farthest point of the garden could be a summerhouse or arbor, acting as a focal point in the view from the house and drawing you down the space to enjoy the reverse view when you look back toward the house, framed by the pergola.

The formal style is endlessly flexible. It can divide a large garden, each balanced room leading to the next and each having a different purpose and layout, both in terms of usage and in the way the detail is carried out. You can move from sitting room to sports room for tennis or any other activity, to swimming room, to play area and so on, all of these framed by hedges, walls or screens of virtually any kind. Arches and pergolas can divide and link areas, avenues of trees frame a vista and draw you down a space, garden buildings and arbors offer a place to sit and so on. Nor need the treatment be necessarily traditional: there are some stunning modern gardens leading out from equally contemporary homes, these also having a regular façade.

A formal layout can look great in a tiny yard, too, with balanced features, planters and ornaments bringing terrific style to the most minimal area. The smaller the space the more important the link between inside and out, and so a color scheme can continue from walls inside to flanking walls on either side outside. Stone paving in a kitchen or dining room can continue into the yard, and there is nothing better than classical urns or statues, of which there is a huge choice these days, for tying the spaces together. Planting too will play its role, with species echoing one another on either side of a doorway or scrambling up matching trellis obelisks. Clipping and control are the order of the day and all this can be remarkably handsome.

The whole character of such places is relatively static, though you can certainly exploit that all-important elements of tension as you approach the next room, the mystery as you wonder what is beyond and finally the surprise as all is revealed, and there is a culmination to the anticipation and each area works as a balanced whole. These are spaces for quiet relaxation rather than boisterous play, unless the rooms are large, but there is a great deal to be said for a measured and structured composition—the style has, after all, been around for a few thousand years and has lasted well.

MODERN MINIMALISM

This is a very cool formal garden which proves the point in the most elegant terms that such compositions do not have to be couched in tradition. Another refreshing aspect is the absolute synergy between interior and exterior architecture; the spaces work in perfect harmony and because of this there is a seamless transition from inside to out. In fact the landscape design takes its cue directly from the building, the clean rectangular pattern of the latter being echoed in the floor plan of the garden.

As in the best gardens the design is essentially simple, but enormously subtle and there is a masterly touch about the spatial dynamics in both the horizontal and vertical planes.

Moving out from the house through floor-to-ceiling glass doors, you enter a broad and crisply detailed terrace with ample room to sit, the focus of which is the cleverly divided pool that stretches away from you. Clipped hedges are used to define the space at a low level while fastigiate trees, which simply take the same type of feature above ground level, help to control the vertical space, as well as providing valuable screening from adjoining properties.

Surfaces are simple and well-proportioned; the materials used being kept to a minimum of paving, water, gravel and grass, all in balance with one another. One of the keys to successful hard landscaping is matching materials to the use to which they are going to be put. Here paving is employed as a backdrop for sitting and pathways, water as a reflective element, lawn as a softer counterpoint and gravel for areas of lesser use, the latter always providing a neutral background that is a perfect foil for the straightforward planting of hedges and trees.

While the main axis reaches away down the length of the garden, over the water, a secondary cross axis that runs across the space is no less important. This is cleverly concealed from the house by the wings of hedge that echo the line of the pool and on the sunny side of the garden there is another crisp terrace that is given over to sitting and dining. Gravel panels give way to a broad step that checks and accommodates the slight change in level and I particularly like the clever contrast of the big and boxy translucent pots, two neutral and two orange.

Where the dining terrace is split between paving and gravel the two pools are bridged by a simple strip of grass, another echo that helps the overall synergy of the various rooms. While the pool closest to the house is still, the one farther away is gently rippled with a bubble jet. The temptation here would be to introduce a fountain which would be quite wrong because it would overdominate; far better to adopt the adage of "less is more" and concentrate on the texture.

Far too few people seriously consider lighting their outside rooms at night, which really does limit the amount of time you can effectively spend in them. When you think about it, this averages out at half a day, spread across the year and the warmer the climate the more this makes sense.

MEASURED BALANCE

Contemporary formality is not a common approach, but it can work beautifully given the right circumstances and a positive touch. Here there is a refreshing sense of purpose, with house and garden in perfect synergy with a combination of paving, planting, water and fastigiate trees.

In this garden illumination has been well thought through, with the sitting and dining areas sensitively lit at both high and low levels. Not only does the scheme work in practical terms, offering illumination just where it is needed for the comfort of its users, but the lights echo the formal pattern of the garden, being regularly positioned throughout the various spaces. This in turn only reinforces the strength of the underlying composition as a whole.

As I've mentioned, formal gardens are not necessarily places for high activity sports—although swimming would be quite feasible here in the larger of the two pools—but why should they be? Every scheme has its purpose and the simple constraints of this design suggest reflectivity and relaxation, which is after all a key function of any outside room. The problem with much of the current design and gardening media is the premise than gardens have to be multi-functional rather than setting out to embrace a single or at least limited number of activities. The fact that this garden does just that in such an elegant way is entirely to its credit.

THE GARDEN PLAN

Formality relies not only on balance and attention to detail but also on the delicate proportion of spaces and their vertical definition. All these criteria need to work in relation to one another as well as taking into account the amount of maintenance that will be required to keep the composition in sparkling condition.

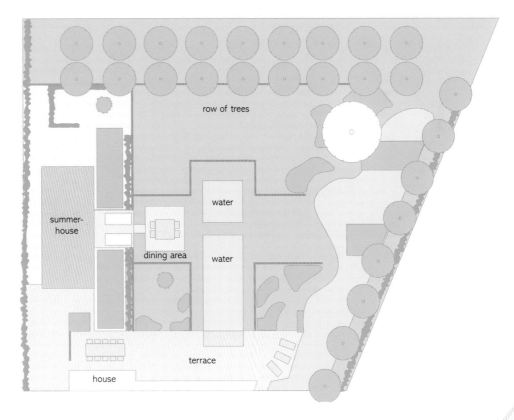

row of trees

summer-house

water

dining area

water

terrace

house

Informal style

In contrast to the age-old pedigree of formal style, informality, on the other hand, is an endlessly flexible style born from modernism and the modern movement. Here things also balance, but in a quite different way, with objects and features of different sizes and volumes complementing each other in different parts of the composition. Imagine the fulcrum I talked about earlier in relation to formal styles, but with weights of different size. These will balance one another, but with the heavier weight close to the fulcrum and the lighter weight farther away, so too with an informal layout, or asymmetry as it is called. In this way, the visual weight of a large terrace on one side of the house could be offset by a group of trees on the other side of the layout, but farther away, or a garden building can be balanced by the substance of a water feature or pergola in a different part of the garden.

Asymmetric gardens too are easily subdivided, and can be completely built up from rectangles overlapping one another and softened with planting, or rather more relaxed with an initial area that links strongly with the house, picking up the lines of the latter, and then becoming progressively softer and looser with strong flowing curves as you move away. Where the first works extremely well in a small garden with a series of intimate spaces, the latter will be excellent where the overall areas are larger and can provide a real

ABOVE LEFT This little circular room is somewhere to get away from it all, surrounded by a combination of stone walls, cleverly framed hedges and plants. The detailing is impeccable and I particularly like the slate inserts within the piers that help to lighten the overall structure.

ABOVE RIGHT This is quite simply floral wallpaper that frames a delightful courtyard. Flower and fragrance, leaf shape, form and texture all combine to create a soft and sheltered envelope that is full of interest. Here is somewhere you could most certainly while away many pleasant hours, and low maintenance too.

RIGHT This is a wonderful working of color, both in terms of the wall and the delicate planting. Sometimes the most contemporary structures are heightened and look even better by the addition of a soft range of species including alliums, iris and the wonderful grass, *Stipa gigantea*. The stainless steel rill adds rippling movement and reflection.

feeling of space and movement, detracting from what are often rigidly rectangular boundaries. Such fluid shapes have in themselves the ability to break sight lines and create hidden areas—there is nothing more attractive and enjoyable than to follow a winding path as it unfolds through the garden, each turn revealing something new and unexpected.

This is not a book about the intricacies of garden design, but about how to use spaces effectively. However, one of the most important tenets in dealing with any situation is to keep it simple and straightforward; over complication is the death of any composition, inside or out. Something else that I learned a few years ago is that what looks right is right. The real point here is having the ability and making time to really look at what you are doing and making a measured decision as to whether or not it works in a

ABOVE Paths that curve away through a garden are always attractive, taking you on a journey through the various spaces. Just what they are made of is almost limitless but this combination of gravel and railway sleepers is attractive and cost effective, acting as a foil to the richly layered borders.

OPPOSITE This is smart and sophisticated and there is always something safe and secure about sitting on an elevated deck, set above the general garden level, in this situation with the pool to one side. The dark furniture picks up the under deck shadows, the latter being accentuated by the open treads of the steps. Soft planting again acts as foil to the architectural character of the room as a whole.

given situation. Design and the sense of knowing what works is not a gift given to a favored few: it is largely common sense that can be built upon with experience and originality, and it is the prerogative of anyone.

There are of course tricks of the trade, but they are obvious when you come to think about them. A long narrow garden is ideal for subdivision; you would not take a path slap down the middle as it makes two even narrower strips and encourages you to run down to the far end! The path should move from one side to the other, then disappear behind a screen before crossing the room again to perhaps give access to yet another space beyond. Another point here is that such a path takes a route far longer than a straight line and so makes the overall spaces feel rather larger than they really are. A variation is to take a zigzag route or use a zigzag pattern with diagonals. Here again we create a feeling of greater space, as a diagonal is the longest available line across a rectangle. All these techniques offer scope for features and furnishings, arches, pools and pergolas, focal points and built-in seating, fire pits and showers: the list is limited only by your imagination and ability to create something utterly personal and unique.

SMALL COURTYARD GARDEN

The smaller and more enclosed a garden is, the greater it relies on its relationship and intimacy with the adjoining house and its place within the immediate surroundings. In this delightful courtyard we have on the one hand the dramatic and unavoidable dominance in the background of an old Victorian mill, complete with soaring chimney and great thrusting gable ends that fill the skyline. Contrasting with this awesome backdrop we have a modern and diminutive town house: The trick is putting these contrasting architectural styles them together in complete harmony, a far from easy proposition.

That this has been successfully achiev is a credit to the designer and owner, who has demonstated a complete understanding not just of the careful linkage of inside and outside space, but the huge potential of utilizing that impressive borrowed landscape view.

This is not an outside room for those w io are faint-hearted, and it's a fact that without a real sense of drama, and bold drama at that, the whole garden could have been hopelessly dominated by the buildings beyond.

The starting place for any garden lies inside the house and an elegantly designed conservatory, which doubles as a dining room, takes you easily outside. In part this is brought about at one level

INTERCONNECTION

An invitation into the first room is irresistible, glimpsed though floor to ceiling sliding glass doors which are framed by plants. The containment of space with a glimpse of what lies beyond is the very stuff of good exterior design. See how the rich and dramatic planting holds the room together.

by the scrambling climbers that soften the ceiling of the conservatory iteself, giving a sense of being in a garden even while indoors. And at ground level the wooden floorboards are aligned with the decking boards that lead away to form the floor of the first outside room. The sliding glass doors, which stretch across the full width of the building, naturally enhance the view, allowing a seamless transition from indoors to out with little or no break, and a truly seductive view when sitting inside. at the dining table.

Once in the garden the view opens up and at a high level embraces the mill with panache, but lower down, and this is the really clever part of this design, one is enveloped within a series of raised beds, the planting of which, particularly

Labels in plan: dining area, shed, decking, conservatory

THE GARDEN PLAN

The two garden rooms are of identical size but handled quite differently. The one closest to the house, floored with decking to lead the eye from the house, is intimately screened with plants while the further dining area is bathed in sun and wide open to the dramatic view of the mill.

dramatic skyline. At a lower level where more detail can be appreciated, annuals add a splash of color while herbs are a must for the kitchen.

The farthest room is more directly open to the view, a sunnier and more expansive place. Here there is somewhere to sit and dine, solid hand-built furniture again being tailored to fit the relatively small space. With a change of room we have a change of flooring, crisp pre-cast concrete paving stones contrasting with a band of cobbles, a change of material indicating a change of use.

Here too is a place for a shed, which is nestled comfortably among the planting, and with a small house every inch of additional storage is valuable. This is a simple enough little building but the thoughtfully selected color and the shiplap boarding provide useful visual links with the textures and finishes used in other parts of the yard and in addition lift it out of the mundane and into an altogether more elegant category.

Plants are again placed in raised beds and planters and the selection of material for both rooms is mercifully simple, with the emphasis on bold foliage rather than a lot of fussy flower. Only a few species are used, but these are cleverly repeated throughout the composition to provide a sense of continuity and togetherness.

The message of this wonderful manipulation of space is simplicity, in terms of both hard and soft landscape. The cliché "less is more" is indiscriminately overused in terms of design, but in this situation it is just right, perfect in fact!

CUSTOM FITTING

Crisply laid decking naturally draws the eye, both toward and out from the building. Most importantly it is aligned with the floor inside, adding to the linkage, which is in turn softened by bold but structured foliage. Glimpsed through the "tension point" formed by the two raised beds a band of cobbles defines the sitting and dining area. Here hand-made furniture is tailored to fit the space while well laid paving proves a stable no-nonsense floor (top left). Built-in seating is a great space saver and cushions add a splash of color. See how the grooved boarding behind the seat provides a visual link with the deck (bottom left).

when you are sitting down, completely hides you from everything beyond; you are safely ensconced in your own secluded world. This is a perfect sitting room, an outside lounge where cleverly designed built-in seating saves valuable space, and climbers, including *Clematis armandii* and Virginia creeper, wrap you about with foliage and enhance the feeling of privacy .

Color has been sensitively used, both in terms of the foliage and the painting of the surrounding structures; it is all of a theme, tying the various elements together and this in turn brings about continuity and allows the overall spaces to feel just that bit more expansive.

The doorway leading out from this first room is deliberately offset, pushing you across to one side to maximize the undisturbed sitting space, and it is flanked by raised beds 2 ft. (600 mm) high. These are boldly planted with the tree ferns and the great strappy leaves of both cordylines and *Phormium*, all of which are tall and powerful enough to partially screen the mill beyond, suggesting that you look up, above eye line to the

WORKING WITH THE LANDSCAPE

In so many gardens that are divided into separate areas the emphasis is on rigid structure and control of the space but here, although there are divisions, they are handled so subtly that there is a wonderful feeling of informality, with one room gently unfolding into the next.

This is a relaxed and relaxing place where you are encouraged to embark on a journey from the intimacy of the sitting area that leads out directly from the house to the furthest reaches of this delightfully sinuous space.

Here the divisions are not the solid structures of walls, trellis or other hard landscape elements, rather the subtle groupings and contrasts of planting that are blended together in different heights, textures and shapes to provide an ever-changing pattern of discovery. Framing is all important here, and each individual room beckons with a classic tension point that takes the form of either an archway or just the delicious narrowing of space where opposing borders lean towards one another, to encourage you onward to see just what lies beyond.

The whole garden rests on a gentle slope that leads up from the house and as you climb the shallow steps from that first paved area those enticing views draw you forward and upward. Formal terracing and retaining walls would be

A SERIES OF ENTICEMENTS

Good views, both up and back down a garden are essential in any successful composition, so the glimpse of a well-chosen planter, framed by a solid wooden archway draws you back towards the house. In the other direction shallow steps and a winding path hint at horticultural joys to come

all wrong here—too hard, too stiff and unyielding —which goes to underline the point that this design is born of sensitivity to the original landform and the potential that it held. There is nothing here that smacks of design for design's sake—quite the opposite—just an understanding of what looks and feels right.

Something else that is beautifully handled in this garden is the whole question of "reverse" views, in other words, when you have been drawn up to the most distant parts of the garden and turn round, the outlook is just as good viewed from the opposite direction. This is important in any garden, whether it is all on one level or set on a slope as this one is, but it is something so many people forget to consider when simply looking away from the house and surveying the garden from that angle.

But this composition functions as far more than just a pretty place; it is a working garden that accommodates both the horticultural joys and skills of its owners and the children and grandchildren

that love to visit. Here is a place in which they can play and explore, and hide around corners, in the deep and mysterious shrubberies and even in a wonderful playhouse that is tucked away from the views of grown-ups. In many ways this is what a true outdoor room is all about, offering a place for everyone and being a space that has the ability to entertain the widest possible range of activities.

Here, much of this is to do with the planting, which is a subtle mix of tough framework shrubs and lower, more delicate and interesting hardy perennials. Evergreens play an important role, adding winter interest and it is so refreshing in this age of somewhat effete planting styles to see rather unfashionable conifers used for what they

CREATING ATMOSPHERE

The interplay of light and shadow is always an important element in perceiving depth in a garden, from a cool sitting area wrapped around by planting to the warmth of a sun-drenched lawn. The sinuous nature of the garden unfolds with waterside planting of hosta, astilbe and iris hugging the stream which flanks the path and in turn gives way to the flowing line of the lawn. Intimacy and detail are also important, and a well-chosen and beautifully laid millstone just brings the paved area alive.

are, sentinels that boldly draw the eye and encourage you into the next room.

While the planting acts as an envelope of year-round color it is the lawn that really holds everything together and it is this sprawling green swathe that carries you from place to place in a celebration of freeform design. Such a complex style is not easy to handle and its success relies on a good eye and an innate understanding of space, something this garden has by the barrowful. The lawn takes its forms from the landscape, acting like a lake or rolling downland and each bay or inlet encloses you for a while to enjoy the delights that each individual place offers, again with its own views back into the main stream of the garden.

As if all these delights are not enough to tempt you further, water, by way of a meandering stream and a series of small pools, adds yet another dimension, which in many a garden would introduce over complication and a restless feel. Here, though, this extra element becomes a natural part of the overall scheme of things, offering a haven for all sorts of wildlife and yet another joy for visiting children.

This is a garden of many different places that caters for many moods— how individual, and how refreshing!

THE GARDEN PLAN

Awkward shapes are difficult, but see how the garden flows from the house, extending into the wider area in a series of flowing curves.

terrace

lawn

stream

Structure

Verticals

Security and the ability to keep people or animals in or out has been a function of outside spaces since time immemorial. Hunters and gatherers started it off with rudimentary boundaries quite literally of sticks and stones, and since then, the perimeters of our gardens have become ever more sophisticated. Mind you, it can be very worthwhile looking at traditional enclosures. I was in a tribal village in Southern Africa a couple of years ago and saw an extraordinarily beautiful fence made up of a double skin of woven branches filled with rocks. This was naturally durable and helped to protect livestock from wild animals. I would not copy this exactly, but it certainly could be interpreted in a thoroughly contemporary way with say colored stone or stainless steel spheres within a framework of painted metal. You should never stop assimilating everything around you.

As well as the boundaries around the outer limits of our garden, there is great potential for vertical structures within the space. Relatively solid, high dividers that break a sight line can be used to form real rooms, but not without the potential of drama. A hedge or wall with a gap or doorway set into it immediately forms a tension point and a glimpse of what lies beyond. If that view is enhanced by a feature in the next room, which could be anything from a well-chosen artwork to an arbor or a pool with a single plume fountain, you have a natural magnet that in turn encourages movement from place to place. Taken a stage further, a hidden entry that could be set between two offset dividers provides even more drama as you have to wait until you are in the next room to see what is going on.

Division can be achieved at any level, and in its way can be all the more tantalizing for it. Water can act as the ultimate divider; you only need a relatively narrow pool to guide you to a bridge or other crossing point. Such a device will not break a view, but it certainly guides you through a space very effectively. All of this points to having an open mind, seeing the possibilities, keeping the spaces fluid and fun. Division is the driver of space, but you are in the driver's seat—make it work.

RIGHT Pierced walls, fences or screens can be remarkably attractive, offering a glimpse of what lies next door. A moon gate can often be walked through, but this is more a porthole into the room beyond, where the mass planting of Japanese blood grass, *Imperata cylindrica* 'Rubra,' provides high drama as it swirls around the standing stones like a red river.

LEFT As a general rule one tries to keep the materials used for dividers the same, for reasons of continuity. Here, however, the designer has made a conscious decision to do just the opposite, with dramatic effect. The tile artwork stands out in sharp contrast against the darker stone, tempting one down the narrow corridor.

BELOW LEFT There is little wrong in using mundane materials for what they are, this is called design integrity. Here corrugated iron sheets make a fine screen, particularly with the scalloped tops that set up a definite rhythm. Here too is a doorway, or frame, to what lies beyond in the form of bold foliage and a jungle set in a wider landscape.

BELOW RIGHT Sometimes an opening within a wall becomes an artwork in its own right and here the cactus is beautifully framed as a three-dimensional image. Apart from offering this picture, the view prevents the internal space from becoming oppressive as well as offering the chance to explore what lies beyond.

Manipulating space

Space, or the impression of space can also be controlled by verticals, particularly fencing. Pale surfaces, and new fencing is often just that, can be glaringly obvious and tend to look closer than it is but, if toned down with a simple stain, will look far more comfortable both on the eye and with planting. It's also true that a slatted fence, using wide boards, brings a boundary in, while thinner, more delicate slats fracture the light and push the boundary away. Plants, too, on a boundary do exactly the same thing; large, bold leaves foreshorten a view while delicate, feathery foliage does exactly the opposite, creating a feeling of greater space. If you think about it this principle works in exactly the same way inside the house, where a heavily patterned wallpaper invariably makes a room feel smaller.

Something we often forget with a solid boundary is the simple fact that there is something beyond it, usually a view. In many cases these are not so good, but there are certainly instances, particularly in a rural situation, where there can be a glimpse of something handsome. In this case you could embrace it wholeheartedly, either by lowering the boundary at that point or leaving a solid section out and replacing it with something see-through.

ABOVE This is just a beautiful wooden screen or fence, washed a pale blue to contrast with the yellow swathe below. This is where imagination comes in and the device is all the more attractive for it. Such a feature is tough and would make an ideal boundary in any garden.

OPPOSITE In a situation where logs are freely available, this makes a terrific wall and is all the more effective when fronted by such a contemporary water feature. There is a great dialogue between the smooth slate and the rugged wood that is accentuated by the use of gray and silver foliage.

Materials and finishes

In many instances your vertical structures may well be already in place, but if not, and you have a choice in the matter, then think about what you can construct them from and the various patterns involved. In basic terms it makes sense to extend the materials used in the house, providing a natural link with the building. Thus brick walls may extend out from a brick house, while stone walls look superb running out from a stone cottage. Wooden homes, of which there are many, would suggest fencing, which comes in a vast range of permutations from boards set horizontally or vertically, to low cost panels or woven sections of hazel or willow. Concrete, which Frank Lloyd Wright astutely called the stone of the twentieth century, is a wonderfully versatile material and you can use blocks which, if smooth faced, can simply be painted, or if rough textured be rendered. Walls that are cast in situ often show the pattern and grain of the boards that acted as the shuttering, or mold, and this too can be attractive.

In reality materials are happy in certain relationships, brick and natural stone, when used as walls, do not sit particularly comfortably together. Brick however is absolutely fine with well-detailed concrete blocks and almost any kind of wood, used in fences and screens. The way in which materials are finished also will have an impact and affinity with their surroundings. Sawn or "dressed" stone is far more architectural in character than a dry stone wall. One would look handsome adjoining a crisply detailed town house, the other more at home within the garden of a country cottage. Exactly the same would apply to a hard smooth engineering brick which has a naturally contemporary feel, whereas a rough, multi-colored old stock brick is perfect in any sort of traditional setting. Much of this is to do with a feeling for materials, a respect for how they look and perform. It is not hard to acquire and in reality means looking, seeing and understanding, which is, after all, the basis of most good and sensitive design thinking.

Whatever the material, if the surface is well finished and durable it can be sensible to leave it in its natural state; honesty counts high in design terms. However, there is often the opportunity to run a color scheme from inside to out, which will naturally link the two areas together. In urban situations where it is impossible to plant through an impenetrable concrete floor and where it would be difficult to provide enough root run in a container for strongly growing climbers, it can look great to paint such climbers on the walls. These could run from outside right back into

the house and, if backed up with potted plants, will provide visual linkage. You can also train or clip plants to frame doors or windows, or even better allow them to dress up or emphasize something like a mural, statue or other ornamentation. The Romans knew all about painting murals, which is just as much fun now as it ever was—have a go!

It is a fact that in a small garden the vertical surfaces can have considerably more area than the floor, sometimes two or three times as much. Again the comparison with the rooms inside our homes comes to mind, but the truth of the matter is that while many people have enormous enthusiasm and style for choosing pictures, hanging ornaments and generally having fun with interior walls their cousins outside often get forgotten altogether. The end result should be originality and making the very best of what you have got. Get friendly with your boundaries; they have a great deal more potential and possibilities than you may think.

ABOVE LEFT The distressed and uneven checkerboard pattern on this wall of gilded copper screens and planters is reflected on the black surface of the pool.

ABOVE Gabions, or stone-filled baskets, were originally used by engineers to stabilize steep slopes. In a contemporary situation, designers have taken to them with a vengeance and they can certainly provide a powerful backdrop, in this case highlighted by the boxed artwork.

OPPOSITE There is little to beat a natural stone wall. It is massive, powerful and brings huge presence to any room. The low wooden bench set in front plays host to earthenware pots that are the perfect complement to the stone, the *Phormium* adding its own sharply architectural line to the composition.

Living structures

Plants alone, whether they take the form of hedges or just a fine border, can act as natural divisions and boundaries in the garden, and character again plays its part. A well-shaped yew, beech or hornbeam hedge is stunning at any time of the year and has the potential to be pierced with an arch or doorway to offer a way to the room beyond. Such species can also be "pleached," whereby a row of trees are trained together to form an aerial hedge, with the stems being kept clean and the tops clipped to a rectangular shape; the effect is dramatic, particularly in formal rooms, where you can see below the canopy but have definition and screening at a higher level. Looser hedges can be planted with many larger shrubs that might include *Rosa rugosa*, bamboo, privet (which when left to flower has the most stunning perfume), *Escallonia*, *Griselinia*, *Osmanthus* and *Symphoricarpos*, the latter two growing in the shadiest of garden rooms.

Low hedges, such as box or lavender will also guide you in a particular direction and parterres have been used in this way for many hundreds of years, often linking into the wider composition of a formal garden. Mazes take this a stage further and you have only to see children picking their way around a maze constructed from brick paths and grass to see how such a simple device can effectively control space.

OPPOSITE You have to remember that when looking at a plan you are seeing things two dimensionally, when the real thing exists in three. There is real verticality here, with the trees pushing upwards between the neatly clipped rectangles of hedging and the cleverly designed hurdles topping the hedge and offering additional privacy.

ABOVE LEFT Hedges form some of the best dividers, and are economic too as the initial cost is low. They can be trimmed to whatever pattern you wish and in this situation control the space perfectly, the scalloped wings in the foreground leading the eye to the tension point of the arch.

ABOVE RIGHT It's fun, but an unusual option, to echo a curving pattern on the ground with a curving support that can allow climbing plants to scramble and lead the eye upward.

Dividers

The reason a small house, or even a large room, can be made to feel larger than it really is revolves around the way in which we manipulate and divide the space. Even in the most high-tech open-plan apartments, most people like to use screens, curtains or other forms of division to simply personalize the place. It comes back to the basic instinct of feeling comfortable and being able to carry out different functions in different places—taken to its extreme it means that we can shelter from that feeling of vulnerability that wide-open spaces can sometimes engender.

Gardens are often larger in area than the house, and so this whole premise makes sense here also, but with the added practical advantages that dividers can also provide shelter from wind, provision of shade and even the creation of a micro-climate that can be a good deal more benign than that outside the boundaries. And the divisions do not always need to be solid. In many instances is is enough to have a low level or slightly higher, but partially transparent, structure that will visually define and separate one area from another, allowing you to designate areas for specific activities.

ABOVE LEFT Poles can be made from all kinds of things, many of them seemingly mundane, but when used imaginatively are full of interest. Wood is a logical choice here, but concrete posts would be far more durable and achieve much the same visual result.

ABOVE Steel reinforcing rods are usually hidden within concrete, but taken out of context and used as a screen take on a character of their own. You could either paint them or allow them to rust to match earthy surroundings.

TOP RIGHT Both concrete and stone can be shaped pretty much how you like and these crisply outlined cubes provide slightly elevated stepping stones across a lushly planted pool.

BOTTOM RIGHT A dark mosaic snake slithering over the surface of a garden doubles as a seat, play surface, table and anything else you can think of. In reality it blends superbly into its drought-tolerant surroundings

Constructing a wooden divider

Rather than buy a screen or divider off the peg why not construct one yourself and therefore personalize the pattern? Make the open panels and diagonally slatted sections to the same widths first and then set the posts in concrete to accept these. The upright adjoining the house can be attached to the latter with expanding masonry bolts. Once the framework of posts is in place screw or nail the panels in position, ensuring that the lower panels are kept clear of the ground to minimize rotting. All woodwork should be treated with a non-toxic preservative prior to planting climbers.

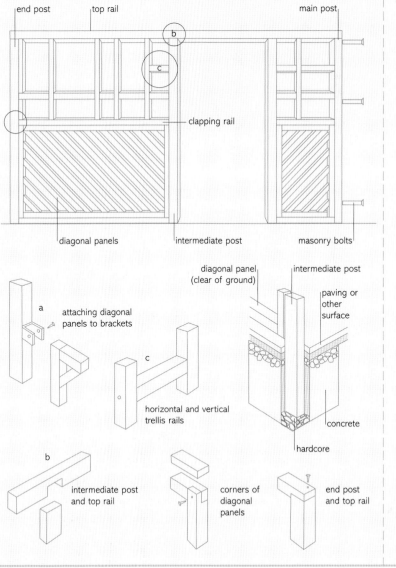

end post   top rail   main post

b

c

clapping rail

diagonal panels   intermediate post   masonry bolts

a   attaching diagonal panels to brackets

diagonal panel (clear of ground)   intermediate post

paving or other surface

c

horizontal and vertical trellis rails

concrete

hardcore

b   intermediate post and top rail

corners of diagonal panels

end post and top rail

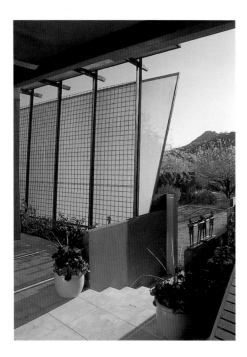

ABOVE In a harsh climate protection from the sun, even when it is climbing or dropping low in the sky, can be essential. The translucent sheet alone might have psychologically seemed vulnerable, but by placing the mesh in front you have a greater feeling of stability.

OPPOSITE The real trick in a small area is to create a feeling of division but at the same time prevent any of the spaces from becoming claustrophobic or too dark. Glass or some other translucent surface is of course the answer and is used here for a screen, together with space-saving built-in seating and soft planting to create a series of delightful outside rooms.

Screens

Of course in a garden, unlike rooms inside the house, dividers have the added advantage of not just controlling space but being a vehicle for plants, and climbing plants in particular. Fragrance, color throughout the year, an ever-changing pattern of flower and foliage can all transform the most mundane division, even a corrugated iron fence, into something quite special. Mind you, don't just write off something like corrugated iron, it's actually durable, can be painted in all kinds of colors, sometimes quite dramatically and is just a good a divider as anything else. This underlines the point of thinking out of context. You will see some brilliant screens and dividers in shops and restaurants, both simple and complex, using all kinds of materials from the high tech to just good old timber. Many of these can be copied or interpreted for use outside.

Much exterior design takes its cue from architecture and interiors, increasingly so, and this makes absolute sense so be aware of the potential of things like toughened frosted glass, stainless steel in many forms, Perspex and plastic. My good friend Paul Cooper, a gifted designer, introduced me to the potential of cricket sight screen material, which is a woven polyester. It is semi-translucent, filters the wind and is as light as a feather; you can roll up and carry a whole screen or fence over your shoulder—fantastic!

And why should screens be static? Think of a long plant trough, or a number of them, with some kind of trellis above. Fit wheels, push them around, position them where you like. By doing this you virtually have a mobile garden and you can certainly reposition the things from time to time to produce an entirely new look to the place. Taken a stage further you could do this with raised beds and even furniture.

Cost too has to be a factor in choosing what materials you use. Walling is expensive, plants relatively cheap, and all kinds of trellis and wooden dividers somewhere in between. A word here about the fashionable trend, largely brought about by half-baked television programs, of painting trellis and dividers one color or another—don't, unless you really know what you are doing. Apart from the fact that you may well have to repaint the thing after just a year or so to keep it smart, and destroy half the plants in the process, think about how a colored screen will effect a planting scheme and the consequent relationship of flower and leaf colors, not an easy one. There is nothing wrong with natural wood, treated against rot if necessary. It weathers beautifully and looks just fine in any situation.

Doorways and entrances

In any room the doorway is often the most important element. Sometimes it is dramatic, shouting at you to come and have a look, sometimes low-key with just a hint of what lies beyond. Either approach is valid and each will have its part to play in the way you use and perceive the overall space.

Entrances are the key to that whole premise of tension, mystery and surprise; they offer the opportunity to find out just what is in the next room, and by so doing have the ability to draw you in a particular direction. This, in overall design terms, is very important. In a formal layout they will be central, or set at points down the main or cross axis. In an informal or asymmetric design they can take you to either side of a space, set up diagonal paths and sight lines, as well as the possibility of zigzagging you from room to room and from place to place. They may be the start and finishing place for paths, a window to a view or focal point, or a solid barrier that physically requires you to open it and step inside.

However casual or formal any such entrances look they need to be thought about at the design stage and positioned accordingly. In any space, inside or out, there are easy and obvious routes to take across a room and in technical terms these are called "desire lines." In reality they are often the quickest option as the crow flies. Sometimes it is good to take these, and in others, as we have seen, there is a valid reason to manipulate space so a greater distance is covered and the room or garden feels bigger as a result.

The type of entrance, as with everything else in the garden, will provide a natural extension of the character of the adjoining architecture. If a house is, say, Victorian Gothic with solid, studded oak doors, then it is natural to use a similar design outside. If, on the other hand, you live in a home with no specific period or style, then the options are greater and you might use wood, metal or simply have an opening or way through with no gate at all.

RIGHT Some places are just downright welcoming and nothing more so than an open door that offers an invitation to see just what lies within. This has a real feeling of the Mediterranean with its color-washed walls, terracotta tiles and water-wise planting.

Gates and doors

Gates and doors are of two basic kinds and as such offer quite different possibilities. Wrought iron or wooden slats will allow a view to run through, to catch a glimpse of what is beyond, which is something that should always be thought about. Just what do you want to see—certainly not an old shed or the back of your neighbor's garage! It should be a good view, perhaps into the distance or alternatively of a well-positioned ornament, seat or water feature. Such features are real magnets and are an important element in the way that we perceive and use space outside.

Solid gates or doors are of course quite different both from the point of view of privacy and completely blocking a view. The great charm of these is that you cannot see what is beyond and there is always that feeling of expectation as you turn the handle, open the door and all is revealed.

Just occasionally, in a tiny yard, you can use false doors to considerable effect. These naturally go nowhere, but can be dressed up with a step and planters to either side with planting round about to give a sense of illusion. Again there is that feeling of what lies beyond, nothing at all, but it's another fun device to help create a feeling of space in a small area.

With any entrance comes a degree of drama which can be dressed up or down depending on the situation, and more important the budget available. In grand garden rooms walls are just the thing, completely

BOTTOM LEFT There is a clever synergy here between the little wicket gate made of stripped poles and the woven retainer of the vegetable bed beyond. Such a gate will not have a long life but if you are clever with wood then a replacement should not be too difficult.

BOTTOM CENTER Gates are as disparate as people; they come in all shapes and sizes, with characters to match. The latter should of course pick up on the overall tone of the rooms it services and a touch of color just gives this elegantly contemporary design a visual boost.

BOTTOM RIGHT Isn't this fun, clever too, with the color of the wooden gate echoing the timber shingles of the piers and adjoining building. Such a gate, being an open structure, provides a view, welcoming you into the garden.

RIGHT I know this garden well, it's tiny and underlines the point that there are many gifted amateurs who beat the so-called professionals all ways up. In such a small space a feeling of what lies beyond is often vital and while this is a mirror it cleverly expands the horizons of this room without being pretentious in any way.

breaking a view. They can be pierced with an arch with a gate within, or if high, swooped down to form an opening which emphasizes the entry point even more. Lower walls, say 3 ft. 3 in. (1 m) high, can be topped with railings or trellis which could in turn be punctuated and echoed by a gate of the same pattern. When the former are softened with planting, the partial view of what lies beyond will be all the more tantalizing.

Planting, on the other hand, is far more cost effective, but no less visually effective. The real difference of course is that while a solid screen can be put up quickly, plants and hedges take a while to get going. Clipped hedges are naturally architectural and the key to success lies in thorough soil preparation with the addition of as much organic matter as you can lay your hands on. The best are certainly yew, beech and hornbeam, these being a lot quicker growing than most people imagine. Entrances can be easily formed, either by simply leaving a gap or training the plants over to create an arch. In a formal room added emphasis could be created with urns or statues to either side, possibly set in niches again clipped from the hedge. Informal ways through a garden are legion and can range from a simple archway smothered in climbing plants to a gap opened in a border, perhaps staggered to hide the view beyond, or a bridge set over water.

TOP LEFT This gate has presence and as such should always be linked in personality to the adjoining garden. Such an entrance suggests a formal layout and its hooped top doubles as an attractive host to climbing plants.

ABOVE The hedges do of course form a natural doorway but the metal arch just provides a little more emphasis, helping to compress the space and of course again offering support to climbers.

TOP RIGHT Color cleverly links gate, arch and door so that we are drawn from one end of the composition to the other between structured beds edged with low hedging. The tall arch has added emphasis and compression, a real tension point before we reach the building.

RIGHT This is a full on moon gate, a good one too, beautifully constructed from stone and offering both a view and entrance into the room beyond, with an inviting path to take you still further. All is softness here, from the loosely planted gate itself, cleverly echoed as a step at ground level, to the grassy bank and ferns nestled against the standing stone beyond.

Constructing metal archways

Metal can be a wonderfully flexible material, albeit one that needs to be shaped or fabricated by an expert to look its best. It is a natural choice for archways, tunnels or pergolas, being hardwearing and available in a wide range of finishes. In this design a reinforcing rod has been uniformly bent and concreted into the ground to form the side supports of a pergola, strengthened by horizontal rods wired in position on both sides and the top.

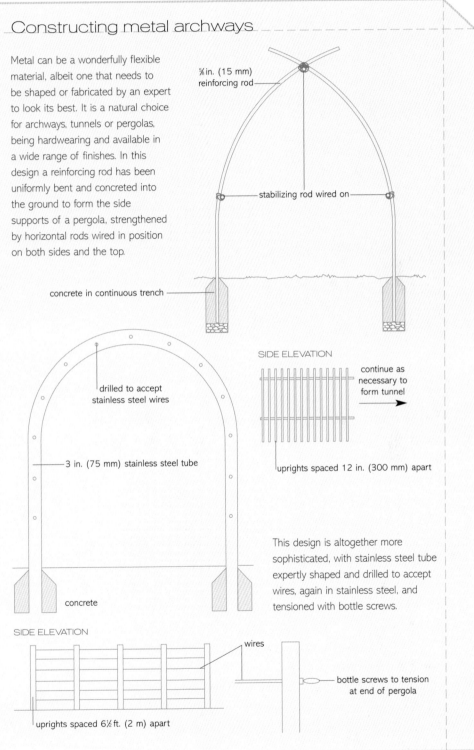

⅝ in. (15 mm) reinforcing rod

stabilizing rod wired on

concrete in continuous trench

SIDE ELEVATION

continue as necessary to form tunnel

uprights spaced 12 in. (300 mm) apart

drilled to accept stainless steel wires

3 in. (75 mm) stainless steel tube

concrete

This design is altogether more sophisticated, with stainless steel tube expertly shaped and drilled to accept wires, again in stainless steel, and tensioned with bottle screws.

SIDE ELEVATION

wires

bottle screws to tension at end of pergola

uprights spaced 6½ ft. (2 m) apart

Ceilings and overhead dividers

It's a reality that few of us really think about ceilings, either inside of outside the house, when in fact they are prime controllers of space. One of the joys of good architecture is the manipulation of volume as you pass from wide to narrow, high to low, large rooms, small rooms, passageways, bright rooms, dark rooms and so on. In shops, restaurants, bars, airports and other public places with particularly high or simply unattractive ceilings you will see all kinds of overhead structures positioned so as to create a new perspective or a different and more comfortable volume. Very often these go completely unnoticed, which is as it should be, but it's fair to say that not many people are aware, or even look up to see what is above them.

Outside things are not really so different, particularly in town where a garden can be surrounded by other buildings that completely dominate the situation. Even where housing is less dense, there are often neighboring windows that look directly into your living space with a subsequent loss of privacy. In high-rise urban settings, walls can soar high above, again with obtrusive windows, and such problems must be addressed.

Just as we have false ceilings in shops, so too can we have them in the garden, although rarely over the whole area. Sitting places are often the most vulnerable, and overhead beams, run out from the house, both help to define vertical space and can break the sight line from those neighboring windows. Keep the design simple: sturdy sawn wooden beams with solid down supports will be fine, and cross wires can be incorporated to allow climbing plants, preferably fragrant, to run over the structure. Paint them a color to link with that used on the house and see if they possibly have the potential for well-planted baskets, above head level, to add color and interest. As with everything, the style of overheads should reflect the room below: rough poles in the Mediterranean, bamboo where there is a Japanese

RIGHT To sit under something, rather than out in the open, naturally gives a feeling of security and seclusion, and if the top is solid it will also keep you dry should the weather turn showery. Cantilevers are always fascinating and here there is a clever piece of construction with the slightly angled roof being supported by stout uprights and a framework of horizontal wooden beams.

influence and high-tech stainless steel in a crisp contemporary room. It can be particularly helpful, with high surrounding walls, to further define verticality with a paint scheme that runs round the yard at the same height as the overheads. As a result your eye is encouraged to stay within this, rather than gaze up into an overpowering world above.

Permanent and semi-permanent structures

Awnings that reel out from the house can be useful for both breaking a bad view and providing shade when needed, while a "sail" can be stretched from an architectural framework of poles for a more contemporary, and more mobile, spin on the same theme. In either case be aware of using linking or contrasting color schemes for just the effect you want.

While many gardens and yards are tiny, many more are considerably larger than the house they adjoin. This means that any ceilings that define vertical space, or features such as arches, arbors, tunnels and pergolas that you can actually pass through, from place to place, will only cover a section or passageway though the area. Some of these features are static, in so much as you sit beneath them to relax, others encourage movement and in themselves become dividers in the overall garden composition. Tunnels, for example, can be fashioned from many tree species, willow, limes and hornbeam in particular, trained to grow together and offering a wonderfully shady way through and between rooms. Long willow stems, or withies, can be literally cut and pushed into the ground where they will sprout and grow away rapidly. Fruit tunnels are rather more architectural, often using hoops of metal, drilled to accept wires that run down the length of the feature. Apples, pears and many other species that have the added bonus of spring blossom can then be trained over the structure so that it becomes a decorative as well as practical element within the overall composition.

Tree canopies can form the most dramatic ceilings of all. The size of tree must relate to the overall space you have available and forest species will be simply unsuitable in a small area for quite obvious reasons, but even in a yard, a well-chosen smaller tree or large shrub will offer shade and screening. This can be an area where an existing plant can be retrained to fulfill a new role. When we moved to our present house I inherited a large overgrown cotoneaster, a bit of a monster really. I took a saw and secateurs to it and spent a good while reshaping the canopy into an evergreen umbrella that in summer is the best place to sit: the ultimate green ceiling.

TOP LEFT Very chic, very crisp with solid overheads echoing the construction of the table below. Plenty of shade here and a natural extension to the building with built-in seating.

BOTTOM LEFT Quite literally a classic room, with stone columns, warm brickwork and an equally warm color-washed wall. The clematis just brings softness and color to the design.

ABOVE Sunken areas can naturally drop the line of a feature into the garden, but always be aware of drainage. Simple overhead slats and built-in seating bring an arbor right up to date, the supports being picked up by the verticality of the stems of the birch trees beyond.

Arbors are freestanding structures within a larger overall garden room; they are intimate places for one or two people to sit. Here you can get away from it all, with a book or refreshing drink, to while away a few hours in peace and quiet, something important in today's ever more hectic world. Style can be architectural or traditional. The real secret is to partially hide them so they can be "happened" upon, tucked back into planting, perhaps found around the turn of a path. As with most things simplicity is the answer: wood or wrought iron are both ideal, forming a framework for climbing plants that will provide fragrance, cast shade and offer privacy. You can buy, or construct if you have a mind to, covered seats, that are a variation on an arbor, these too can be nestled into a quiet corner or perhaps used in a formal layout, facing one another across a garden.

Pergolas

Pergolas are really a series of arches joined together and perhaps the most important thing is that they should have somewhere positive to go. I have visited so many gardens where the thing simply leads to a shed, compost heap or something else equally unsatisfactory. As with all design, form follows function—an ornament or seat as a focus, a cross axis in the middle to offer a journey in another direction or simply the promise of something unforeseen at the far end. Pergolas can offer real feeling of tension, bursting out into a new room or offering tantalizing glimpses of the garden to either side. I could write an entire book on pergolas I have seen and hated—for goodness' sake keep the thing simple, you don't need convoluted carpentry that is plainly ostentatious. Also be sure to make them generous; the ones you buy off the peg are too small, both in height and width and allow little room for climbing plants to fully develop. There is nothing worse than being lacerated by a climbing rose that droops from above. If you want to see decent pergolas look at old garden books, where you will see substantial brick or stone piers linked by solid wooden beams dripping with flower and foliage.

ABOVE LEFT Roofs can make intimate rooms, particularly when given shelter and protection from an often glaring sun by means of a ceiling. The views of course can be staggering and there is little problem with plants provided you understand the inclement conditions and provide adequate depth of lightweight compost.

ABOVE RIGHT Overheads, beams, tubes and wires are all vehicles for planting that can climb and scramble over their surface. In an urban situation they provide invaluable screening from overlooking windows of adjoining properties.

RIGHT Highly stylized and highly personal, great if you like this kind of treatment. It all goes to show that exterior decorating, like its cousin inside, is all in the eye of the beholder.

Making a wooden pergola

The key to pergolas is simplicity; don't overdo them, and remember they are a vehicle for climbing plants, which are the real stars. Don't be afraid to use stout wooden beams to form both the uprights and top members. Give them generous proportions with ample head room for the tallest people, bearing in mind the working height will probably be reduced by about 2 ft. (600 mm) when a tumbling climber is fully established. Wires will be useful to tie plants in and for maximum durability, concrete the posts firmly in the ground.

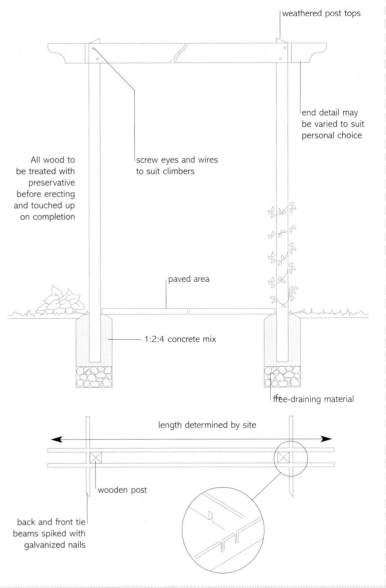

weathered post tops

end detail may be varied to suit personal choice

All wood to be treated with preservative before erecting and touched up on completion

screw eyes and wires to suit climbers

paved area

1:2:4 concrete mix

free-draining material

length determined by site

wooden post

back and front tie beams spiked with galvanized nails

Surfaces

Most people are pretty good at choosing carpets: they match them to their overall color schemes, use them as a linking element throughout the house and allow them to highlight specific areas. Carpet shops and large garden centers or stone yards are really not so different—there is a huge selection to choose from. But while many of us use restraint and common sense inside, I'm afraid it's often quite the reverse in the rooms outside. The range is quite staggering, and increases every year, which leads to the real problem of too much choice and subsequent over complication. I have said time and time again that in all areas of design the simple things work best, and this is nowhere more apparent than in the garden.

One of the most important things to remember is that the surface, or hard landscape, generates the bones of the layout: it will frame areas, provide floors for specific purposes and form paths. Skeletons are made from a single material and while you can mix and match surfaces in the garden to a degree, don't go overboard or the result will be a mess.

We have already talked about linking interior and exterior space, and floors are one of the best ways of achieving this. Terracotta inside and out, fine old stone flags in a hallway leading to a path from the front door, stripped floorboards giving onto a deck. All these reinforce the bond and allow house and garden to flow rather than exist as separate entities.

Where you are thinking of creating a large floor the general rule of hard landscaping is that one material, say a good-quality pre-cast paving, can become rather too heavy. Three surfaces on the other hand will be too busy while two, of which one dominates, will often be perfect. Taking this a stage further, it is naturally sensible if the materials echo those used in the building. A fine old brick-built house may have stone floors, so what is more natural than to use the same stone outside, but with a number of slabs omitted and filled in with brick, of a similar color to that used in the walls. The stone will cover the majority of the area, but the brick will bring in a little mellow softness and counterpoint, striking just the right note.

RIGHT The floor of your garden will probably receive more wear than any other element which means it must be carefully selected in relation to the overall design and correctly laid. One thing is certain; you have many choices, so restraint is paramount. Here a cast concrete path offers a flexible route through the space, contrasting well with the smooth black cobbles and bridging the water to either side.

LEFT Contemporary formalism is hot news at the moment and there is no doubt that such compositions can look undoubtedly chic. There is an assured crispness of the carefully detailed pool, rill and steps, the whole arrangement set off by wonderfully moody borders.

BELOW This could be a tricky one in stiletto heels and the table is carefully positioned on solid sections. The theme is fun though, and the galvanized grids help build up an interesting pattern that links with the raised bed on one side, where the strong color draws the eye and brings the planting in, and the pool on the other.

BELOW RIGHT Random stepping stones, although carefully positioned, can take you on a meandering route, whether it be through a lawn, gravelled area, planting or, as here, across water. Set the slabs on solid black piers to that the visually "float" above the surface.

Selecting materials

Materials exist in "families," which are broadly split between natural and synthetic. In most instances families should stick together; they look and feel more comfortable that way. On the natural side we have stone, gravels, sand, wood, cubed granite called setts, cobbles, boulders and so on. The character of each of these can be further developed by the way in which they are treated. A rough-hewn stone with a riven finish is more traditional than the same stone sawn into crisp modules, which has a contemporary feel. One will be comfortable wrapped around a period home, the other happy in a high-tech steel and glass situation. One of the best ways to understand the synergy of natural materials is to look at Japanese gardens, where they are blended and juxtaposed with huge sensitivity and skill.

Man-made surfaces are legion and include pre-cast and in situ concrete, block paving, steel, iron, glass beads and so on. Plastic has been frowned on, largely due to horticultural snobbery, but materials such as artificial turf, available in a wonderful range of colors, is nothing more than waterproof carpet and should be treated as such. It is fantastic for roof gardens and the like where it can be cut to any shape that takes your fancy, and set with a deck or rainbow colored glass beads for stunning effect.

Laying a cobbled cartwheel

The first job is to lay the outer brick edging to a perfect circle, the center of which is a large white cobble, bedded in mortar over a foundation of 4 in. (100 mm) of well-compacted hardcore or crushed stone. This foundation is carried right across the circle and surrounding paving, with the contrasting cobbles carefully set in a mortar bed. This is a careful and time-consuming job and to make life easier you can work around a template made from wood that conforms to the shape of the pattern of the black stones. Once these are in place and the mortar has set you can remove the template and fill in the rest of the pattern.

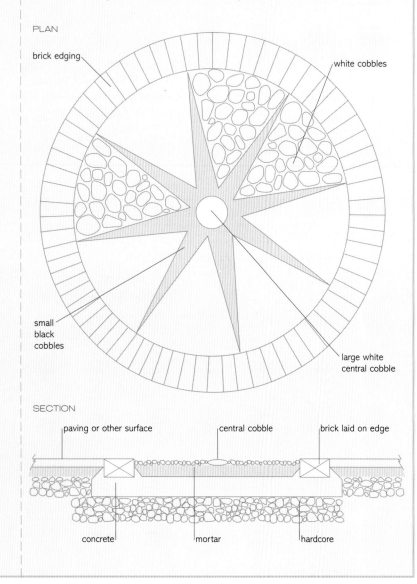

PLAN

brick edging

white cobbles

small black cobbles

large white central cobble

SECTION

paving or other surface

central cobble

brick laid on edge

concrete

mortar

hardcore

Small units

TOP FAR LEFT You just cannot
beat natural materials for their
organic feeling of permanence.
Each module of the path is slightly
different in length and thickness,
but the overall design has a strong
linear pattern. Gravel is the perfect
counterpoint, being small enough to
fill in the area perfectly and acts as
a neutral background.

BELOW FAR LEFT This is
painstaking work and takes time.
It's also idiosyncratic in that this is
a personal feature set in a garden
with a particular theme. Such a
feature has a long history and many
of the earliest gardens contained
cobbled patterns on a similar vein.

LEFT Strong color needs careful
handling and this deep red gravel
is a particularly personal choice,
forming both stepping stones
and larger areas of flooring. The
contrasting combination of the
echeverias and grasses sets
up an interesting dialogue in this
garden of circles and curves.

Wooden flooring

Wooden flooring has been incredibly popular over the past decade or so, and deservedly so; it's an incredibly versatile surface. In a more contemporary situation a wooden beach-side home is just asking for decking, but equally a crisply detailed paving could blend perfectly with clean railway sleepers that form both part of the floor and surrounding raised beds. In other words it's all about sensitivity, self-control and having an understanding of the various materials that are at your disposal.

The modular size and shape of any material will, or should have, a real bearing on the way that it is laid. Just as large slabs of stone or pre-cast concrete lend themselves to overall rectangular layouts rather than circles or curves, for the simple reason that cutting then to such shapes is both costly and time-consuming, wooden decking, laid in planks, will inevitably give a geometric, sharply angular feel to any design in which it is used.

ABOVE LEFT There are two basic materials here, wood and metal, the latter in the form of grids that both lead the eye to the pool and frame it. In such an architectural situation, the planting needs to be equally bold, *Phormium* and palms taking center stage.

ABOVE Here is a situation where the design of the handrails mimics that of the deck boards, the whole effect being enhanced by a complex shadow pattern—really rather cool!

RIGHT There is a lovely relationship here between the austerity of the design, with its basis of clean-lined wooden boards, and the wonderful eccentricity of the wall-hung artwork. As with many contrasts, the one makes the other all the more telling.

Steps and levels

Rooms, unless very old, seldom slope in a house, but the ones outside often do and in consequence need rationalizing in some way. This in part can be handled with steps or ramps, but in certain situations the whole garden can be made up of a series of level platforms that work their way up or down a gradient. Here again, the choice of surfacing will be important and decks, which can be built out over a slope, linked with steps, will be far easier and cheaper to construct than paved platforms that will need serious foundations, retaining walls and have engineering implications.

As a general rule steps should always be as wide and as generous as reasonably possible. There is a classic dimension that is particularly easy to climb which states that the rise should be 6 in. (150 mm) and the tread, the part you put you foot on, 18 in. (450 mm). Materials for steps should take

ABOVE These broad and impeccably detailed wooden steps almost seem to float up the slope, giving way to an equally sophisticated and ample sitting area at the top of the rise.

TOP RIGHT Railway sleepers are a handsome constructional material and if used more than two courses high need to be bolted together securely as well as to be pinned into the ground. The pale pre-cast concrete slabs and steps contrast well with the darker timber.

BOTTOM RIGHT There is nothing terribly complicated here, just a well put-together flight of steps that allows easy access between the two levels, softened by bold foliage.

Constructing sleeper steps

The key to this flight is the fact that the sleepers, or they could equally be long logs, are staggered. This gives them inherent lateral movement rather than climbing the slope in a straight line. Construction is very simple and involves cutting slots into the slope, thoroughly compacting the ground below and firmly pegging the sleepers in position. The addition of smooth boulders and planting, which could include sprawling thymes between the steps, completes the picture. For a slightly more architectural approach pre-cast concrete slabs, bedded on mortar over a suitable foundation of hardcore, act as wide treads set between the sleeper risers for a crisp contrast of materials.

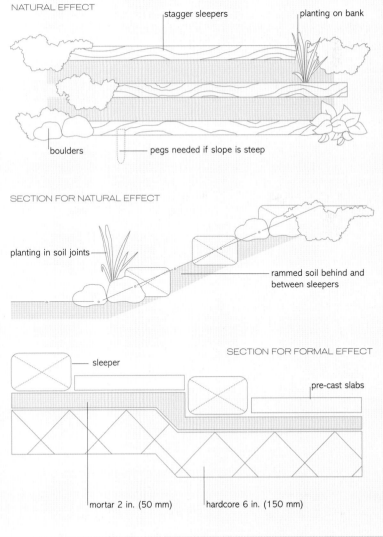

NATURAL EFFECT

stagger sleepers

planting on bank

boulders

pegs needed if slope is steep

SECTION FOR NATURAL EFFECT

planting in soil joints

rammed soil behind and between sleepers

SECTION FOR FORMAL EFFECT

sleeper

pre-cast slabs

mortar 2 in. (50 mm)

hardcore 6 in. (150 mm)

their cue from those used elsewhere: stone paving suggesting stone steps, brick to brick, wood to wood and so on. Smaller modules conform to free-form or curving shapes more easily, while gravel and cast concrete can take up virtually any shape you like. The texture is also important: a riven or uneven floor is better suited to a sloping path where greater grip is useful. Consider also the visual impact of the units you use. A brick is longer than it is broad so laid across a path or step it will slow you down but laying it down a pathway, with the joints running away from you, will have the opposite effect, speeding you up and drawing both feet and eye along the pattern.

FAR LEFT This wooden path is made up of
an abstract pattern of thick boards sunk flush
with the lawn. This should be of hard rather
than soft wood for a long life but just be
careful when mowing and sink the boards
just a little deeper than the lawn if needs be.

LEFT The bands of stone set between grass
define the way to the seat and small sitting area.
The fact that the strips are set at unequal
distances adds a little interest to the pattern.

TOP LEFT This reminds me of the back of a
snake and there is no doubt that there is a
strong directional emphasis here. Halfway down
the paving broadens out, a device to draw you
towards another path set at right angles.

ABOVE Quiet and expansive formalism is
heightened by the planes of decking, gravel
and grass. Even the way the lawn is precisely
mown adds to the geometry of the surfaces.

Lawns and living flooring

But of course not all floors are going to be paved, and soft surfaces in the
form of lawns and ground covers are also applicable and a good deal
cheaper and easier to install than their hard landscape counterparts. Blades
of grass and small plants come into the small module category and can easily
take on curving and free-form patterns. Grass is only one choice, albeit a
hard-wearing one that grows in most parts of the world, and one that will
tolerate a range of conditions, from full sun to anything other than the
deepest shade. Plants such as chamomile, thyme and moss are somewhat
less durable but can all have their place, the first two having the added
advantage of being fragrant when crushed underfoot. They can also
incidentally be used for occasional seats, although only in dry weather!

In some of the most elegant and subtle compositions for outdoor rooms
I have seen there is usually at the basis a delightful blending of hard and
soft flooring surfaces, which bring color, interest and harmony, some of
the most important ingredients for bringing any garden alive.

Decoration

Light and shade

In gardens and yards, night lighting is almost taken for granted these days, albeit not always installed for the best or most subtle effect. Lighting your outside space at night naturally extends the amount of time you can use your garden for a whole range of activities, which has to be good. There are, of course, an increasing number of ever more inventive ways that you can do this, but lighting is generally divided between practicality—which will illuminate doorways, sitting areas, the way to a garage, utility space, paths, steps and other similar features—and decorative techniques that bring specific areas and focal points to life in a very different way.

But with the prevelance and increasing sophistication of artificial lighting, most people, including many modern garden designers, have forgotten the importance of sunlight and the magical shadows it creates. Time was, not so long ago, that electricity was unknown, but this did not prevent garden owners of the past using sun and shade to create wonderful effects.

The bright light countries of the Mediterranean and Middle East have been the cradle of gardens for millennia and here people fully understood, and still do, the counterpoint that can be achieved by the careful positioning of a tree, canopy or building. Those wonderful Italian cypresses lining a classic formal garden with hard black shadows stretching out across a lawn or courtyard have the ability to divide space just as effectively as a physical screen as you move from light to shade and back again. Such a pattern cast across a space will tend to slow you down, while several shadows running down the length of a vista will do just the opposite, urging you onwards to a further point. The sun, of course, swings across the sky throughout the day and shadow patterns are ever changing, something that can bring great subtlety to a composition.

In an orchard, or under the canopy of a woodland, a carpet of light and shade will be cast on the ground, gently moving with the slightest breeze and even in the smallest of outside rooms this same effect can be achieved to utterly charming effect with just a single well-chosen and positioned tree.

RIGHT The cool shade of a porch is just the place to be in summer, dappled sunlight filtering through the tree above, which in itself forms a positive link between house and garden, with the foliage brushing the canopy. A single seat is just for one; it's good to be alone sometimes.

LEFT The Italians have always had panache as well as a relaxed attitude to the garden. This perfect dining room set in a courtyard gives out from broad doors and is shaded by the wisteria-smothered metal overheads. The planting is confined to those glorious pots.

BELOW LEFT Verandah, cloister, call it what you will, this area is cool and shaded, forming a restful walk beneath the eaves at the rear of the house. Look at how solid and sturdy the supports are—they are not just strong but bring real visual stability to the place.

BELOW RIGHT This could only be an English country garden, the old tree with its seat casting dappled shade across the lawn before moving into sunlight and then into the borrowed landscape of the meadow beyond.

Beams, awnings and other overhead structures will also naturally cast shade, and by creating areas of coolness tend to define their own space to which people will be naturally drawn on a hot day.

Perhaps the greatest invention known to man is the verandah, prevalent in the southern states of America and much beloved by the Victorians in England, and still a vital outside room in hot climates, where it can be used as an extra bedroom in the hottest months. It is a delicious halfway house between inside and out, where you can relax in a pool of shade, preferably with a drink, while contemplating the baking heat a few feet away.

For practical purposes, artificial lighting is, of course, important. With steps, for instance, you do not want a light on a pole that simply illuminates the top of your head; you need it at ground level, perhaps built into the flight itself so that you can clearly see where you are going. A pretty good rider is the fact that it is the light that is important and not the fitting, meaning that

ABOVE Lighting is, or should be, an art form and both the lights and battered stone walls are a modern rendition, reminiscent of Frank Lloyd Wright's work. The point of course is that both sit comfortably together, the angled tops of the lights completely at home with the stonework.

OPPOSITE This is all pretty special, from the uplit cantilevered steps to the tight shafts of light set in the sides of the swimming pool. The real point here is that this lighting scheme has been thought of as a complete entity and not assembled piecemeal over a period of time; as a result it works just as well, perhaps better, than something inside the home.

the latter can in most instances be hidden or at least be unobtrusive. If you are creating a series of rooms or outside spaces then there is natural potential to light each, perhaps in a different way. Here again you can take your cues from inside the house and while you might not want chandeliers hanging from the trees, you can certainly use uplighters, downlighters, spotlights, floodlights, wall lights and fairy lights. Safety, as ever, is important and electricity is dangerous, particularly when mixed with water. Always enlist a professional electrician, versed in exterior use.

Focus lighting

Ways in and out of the house, together with entry points between garden rooms, are a natural focus, as are arbors, summerhouses and other sitting places. An urn or statue, backlit and glimpsed through a doorway, can be breathtaking. Planting takes on an altogether new dimension when lit from beneath, quite different from sunlight from above. Here you see the shape of a species from the ground up, which can be full of drama. Trees can be wonderfully lit in the same way, lights being set at ground level with a tight beam picking out all the fissuring on the trunk and branches above. This same technique of grazing light can be used on the face of a building to highlight brickwork or wooden cladding. Spotlights will pick out a feature in sharp relief while a floodlight casts a wider, warmer beam, illuminating an area rather than a specific object. Backlighters on the other hand are tucked up close behind a statue or ornament, providing a silhouette. One of my favorite techniques is "moonlighting," where a number of low wattage bulbs are placed high in a tree, shining down onto a flat surface such as a lawn or pavement. In this way the shadows of branches are projected onto the ground to form a tracery of moving patterns on the floor below.

Just a word here about security lighting, which is increasingly important around many homes. Very often very bright halogen lamps are fitted, and while these certainly illuminate a wide area they will also blind you if you look directly at them. In addition to this people can stand in the dark pools of shadow beneath them and be practically invisible. The current thinking is to use a number of lower-powered lights that can cover the same area but are easier on the eye and provide a better spread of clearer illumination.

Remember that lighting is eye-catching and as a result it should be used carefully, sparingly and with sensitivity for the best effects. Your outside rooms are not Coney Island—use restraint and common sense!

Feature lighting

LEFT In a small garden there will be only room for a limited number of focal points, and as such they will have to be carefully positioned and if possible perfectly lit at night. This water slide would be all but invisible in the dark but being lit from within it simply glows, the water taking the beam down into the water.

BOTTOM LEFT Modernist plate glass panels march up the slope, being superbly lit from below. Thick glass, like water, has the ability to transmit light through the length of the feature, the top edges being brightly illuminated, something that picks them out in sharp relief against a dark background.

RIGHT A subtropical garden at dusk with the palms lit with "grazing" beams from below so that all the textures and irregularities of the trunks are brought alive. Plants, features and trees look totally different bottom lit, as we are so used to see them during daylight hours, illuminated by the sun above.

Furnishings and incidental features

I've talked about all kinds of things in this book and hopefully they will provide you with the tools to create a series of outdoor living spaces that are just right for you. But in exactly the same way as a new house is devoid of character when you first move in, so too will be your garden. We have discussed the fact that is personality—your personality—that makes a place just right for you, whether it is inside or out, and in all probability your sense of taste will follow suit. In other words, if you have a fondness for traditional art, architecture and ornament, these same likes will extend into all areas of your home. If on the other hand you have a thirst for all things new and contemporary, then your exterior rooms will also mirror this.

Most of these will be movable, such as freestanding furniture, statues, pots, parasols and all kinds of ornaments. Some on the other hand will be an integral and permanent part of the overall room, including built-in seating, tables and water features. While the latter will almost certainly be part of the initial design process the others may well be brought in at the final stages and the danger, as with furnishing and decoration inside the home, is one of over complication. Some people have a special knack for dealing with eclecticism and can fill a space with a seemingly incomprehensible array of ornaments that manage to look just right together; others lack this finesse and need a more controlled approach.

While furnishings do indeed reflect personality and the overall style of the place it will be almost inevitable, and naturally acceptable, to build up a collection over a period of time. The problem very often can be that you get a little too close to your living spaces and it sometimes needs a fresh eye, and this is something I'm called on to do a lot, to take a hard look at things and be a little ruthless in sorting out the wheat from the chaff. Tough but necessary, as I'm sure many of you will know!

RIGHT Some features create a focal point about which the whole garden revolves and there is enormous movement in this Nautilus snail seat that wraps itself around the palm. The pattern is continued in the paving at ground level, with a combination of a rippled stone spiral interspersed with cobbles tightly packed together, just as they should be.

LEFT This is different: a little rill runs along the back of this long seat that would sit a couple of dozen with ease and certainly be a wonderful place for children to play, both messing about with the water and jumping up and down off the woven cushions, which can easily be brought under cover if it rains.

TOP LEFT I'm never quite convinced by these: they are fun but only last a limited time owing to the fact that the woven stems get eaten by squirrels. They also give you a very damp rear end even after a light night-time dew, but it does bring focal point status to the old fruit tree with its interweaving scrambling rose.

TOP RIGHT Sunken gardens and areas can be terrific fun, but mind the drainage—they can rapidly fill up with water if there is nowhere for it to go. This is a little slot of a place with a feeling of compression at you approach the built-in seat at the end. Remember when sitting here that the reverse view must be just as good.

Built-in seating

The range of available furniture is staggering, as any visit to a garden center will testify, but before you buy the first thing that comes to hand, do consider the advantages of actually constructing pieces rather than buying them off the salesfloor. In this way you can not only link them into the overall pattern of your outside room, but they can double as storage, play surfaces and a good deal of other things. Such furniture can act as an extension of the house, running out from the building or enclosing a space and aligned to a paving grid which will visually "lock" it into position. What would be more natural on a deck than built-in benches, with hinged tops for storage within, and a solid table as a centerpiece to the area? Similarly, a floor that is laid with crisp pre-cast slabs might suggest seating built from rendered concrete blocks with a seat of the same paving, cushioned with squabs and cushions that could pick up a color scheme from elsewhere.

Raised beds are in reality built-in seats with the tops left off and if they are constructed to the same height, approximately 18 in. (450 mm), then they will be at perfect perching height. Always make them of ample proportions with adequate drainage; the bigger the bed the greater volume of soil and the better the growing conditions. In a small garden, raised beds can be invaluable to boost plants and get them up onto walls and fences quickly.

Room sets

RIGHT This is a bit like a school cafeteria, albeit rather more sophisticated and whoever set this out knows a thing or two about etiquette. It looks very smart indeed and the terrace is large enough for plenty of guests. The really humorous thing is the cow coming round the corner; they really do play havoc with the lawn.

BOTTOM RIGHT This is comfy: nice deep chairs, a blocky little table, red wine and grapes set delicately on hosta leaves. It's a lovely little outdoor room with box clouds in the pots and a railing guarding the steps down to the lower garden—very good.

OPPOSITE This companionable grouping of deep, comfortable-looking chairs and stools-come-tables is given a feeling of seclusion by tucking it behind the planting set into the center of the courtyard. It is the type of furniture that readily moves from indoors to out on fine days.

BELOW LEFT This just welcomes you to a sunny afternoon spent chatting or reading. The table and chairs are easily moved and the overhanging roof provides shade. The point here is that there is nothing fancy, just common sense; many gardens would be the better for it.

BELOW RIGHT Dappled shade is delightful over a sitting area and these chairs and table are easily folded away when not in use, also being light enough to be repositioned around the garden whenever you want.

OPPOSITE This has to be one of my favorite photographs in the book, really because it's so ordinary. There is no over design here, in fact things are a little scruffy, which just adds to the charisma. If you have space this is just the sort of thing you should use it for.

Freestanding furniture

Freestanding furniture comes in all shapes and sizes and while some of us like a matching set, it can be equally good to pick up tables and chairs from anywhere and just mix them up with abandon—it's your place after all. One word of advice: Much garden furniture is amazingly uncomfortable and imitation cast iron chairs with floral patterns, in particular, has the ability to leave an imprint on your bottom. In other words, try before you buy.

Fabrics outside naturally tend to take a good deal of wear and need to be chosen accordingly. Awnings and seat covers can be made from canvas, and there are fabrics that are specially waterproofed for exterior use. These are particularly good for bean bags, which are irresistible to children and dogs alike. In my book, hammocks come about as close to heaven as you can get. I personally don't like those that come with an immensely heavy frame—they are just too unwieldy—but stout fixings for your portable variety are essential. Here, too, you can have fun with colored fabrics: either match them into your overall scheme or just go wacky for an individual statement.

Water features

Raised pools are a variation of raised beds, being built in much the same way but incorporating waterproofing in the form of a butyl liner or rendered concrete with a suitable additive. Such pools are naturally rather safer for youngsters than something at ground level, but awareness and sensible precautions are always the order of the day where water is involved. Water features, other than ponds or pools, cover a wide spectrum which is being added to on a nearly daily basis. Nearly all of them will form a focal point so their positioning is very much an integral part of the overall design. Most of these are what I call "closed" features, in that there is no visible open water, and work on the principle of a buried tank within which piers are built, or a framework is available to support the feature above. This can be anything from a smooth drilled boulder surrounded by loose cobbles and planting, to a millstone or glass or stainless steel structure. A submersible pump then circulates water through the feature in a continuous cycle. Maintenance is straightforward and really amounts to keeping the pump filter clean and ensuring there is always ample water in the reservoir.

Wall-hung water features are also widely available and while these have tended to be cherubs or other unlikely classical features, there is now a far wider and more contemporary palette available—just keep your eyes open or even think of constructing something yourself to your own taste.

ABOVE These are waterworks on the grand scale with ornamental pools flanking the walls and a swimming pool in the foreground. The spouts are fun though and are easily constructed with pipes leading back from the pool that are connected to one or more submersible pumps.

TOP RIGHT It's the sound of falling water on a hot summer's day that would be so attractive in this situation and the terracotta tiles and color washed walls add warmth to the composition. Careful with the architectural plant in the background, it's giant hogweed. It's good looking but can bring you out in a very nasty rash.

BOTTOM RIGHT Great spouting snakes! Tons of fun and they work in exactly the same way as the other features on this page. Remember that with any running water you are going to get a degree of evaporation, so top up as necessary or to reduce maintenance even more fit a float switch that does the job automatically.

Making a water chute feature

I picked up this old water gutter hopper in a reclamation yard and positioned it in a client's garden over a small raised pool. The latter is lined with butyl and you will see that I have carried this into the wall and up between the brickwork so that it is completely concealed at water level. A submersible pump is taken through the liner and sealed accordingly, then through a drilled hole in the screen wall and up so that it empties into the hopper, where it gushes back into the pool. Because the outlet pipe is a large diameter I restricted the flow in the vertical section just to slow things down a bit.

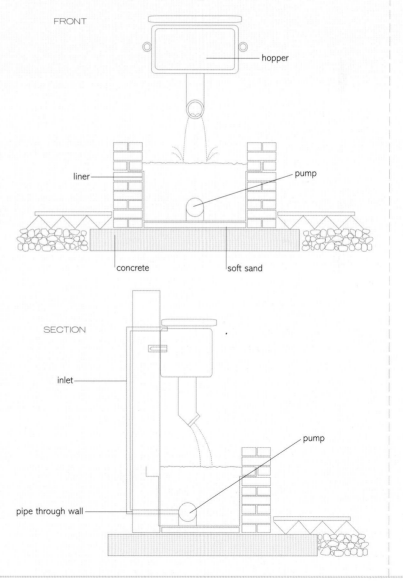

Making a fountain feature

This is the prototype for a whole range of what I call "pump and sump" water features. The principle is simple enough and uses a tank, either sunk in the ground, as in the vase shown below, or within a raised bed, as shown in the top artwork. Within this you construct piers to carry whatever the feature may be—a millstone, smooth slate or drilled boulder. A submersible pump is placed in the bottom of the tank and a pipe run through the feature so that water can bubble over the surface. Fill the tank, connect to a power supply—always installed by a reputable professional to keep safety in mind, and away you go.

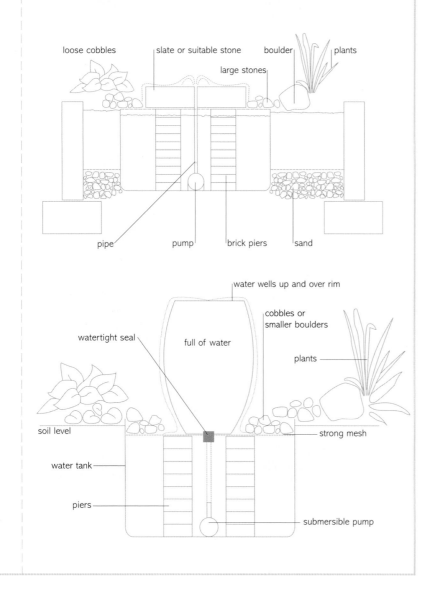

Fountains

FAR LEFT TOP The reflectivity
and smoothness of stainless steel
has made it a favorite material
amongst contemporary designers.
In this case water wells up from
within the circle and spills over the
edges to be returned to the sump
to be recycled once more; white
gravel making a very effective
contrast to the dark water.

FAR LEFT BOTTOM This is
a neat little feature, operating
with a pump set in a pool below.
The reconstituted stone bowl is
precisely cut with a lip that throws
a delicate stream of water into the
pool. With any feature of this kind
you must ensure that the bowl is
perfectly level to maintain the flow.

LEFT Is it a shower, a water
feature or both? It doesn't matter
really, it would certainly work as
either but the real attraction is
in the ingenuity of how it's put
together with bent copper sheeting
and pipe work. Beneath the water
curtain lies a butyl liner or concrete
shell that directs the flow into
the stream and from there
away down the garden.

Stream and rills

BELOW This broad rill is full of ripples and movement, sending a cascade down to the lower pool where a submersible pump recycles the water back up to the higher level to flow round the system again.

RIGHT Narrow rills are often faster running and I love the asymmetry of this one, recessed to one side of the cast concrete retaining wall. It also cleverly suggests an irrigation channel in an otherwise arid situation.

OPPOSITE Water is the entire focus of this garden, sliding down a sheet of stainless steel and through a channel which is bridged with solid wooden blocks set on a slight radius. The circular pool acts as a backdrop to planting that runs back to the solid stone gabions.

Decorative devices

And then of course there are all the incidentals, such as mirrors, murals, *trompe l'oeil* paintings and all the rest. Such things certainly have their place, but be careful and just be aware of the potential, or otherwise, of each. Mirrors can be fantastic in a small yard to increase a feeling of space or bring reflected light into a dark area. Site them carefully though, angled into planting or set into a false arch facing across the room. You don't put them at the end of a path to say hello to yourself on the way down—that's a bit obvious! Sculpture can range from a fine antique or a bespoke commission from a contemporary artist to a found object, which might be a gnarled old branch or an ancient grindstone. The important thing is that they are both well sited and personal to you: at the end of a vista, glimpsed through an arch or at the turn of a path where they guide you in a particular direction.

Finally, a word on ostentation—don't. Those *trompe l'oeil* things really are pretty useless and smack of over-expensive city gardens. They usually fool no one and are simply design for design's sake. A fine mural on the other hand, which can look real, humorous and most things in between, can be stunning and bring a yard alive in a completely unique and personal way. Let your imagination run wild: what might you do?

BELOW LEFT The fern etched into the background panel makes a subtle and effective garden decoration, picking up the same growing species used elsewhere. I believe that art should be used far more to enliven outdoor rooms; it can be extremely attractive.

BELOW CENTER This is eclectic art at its best, both of these features being homemade. The highly individual arch, which would be better than most to host a climbing plant, frames the glass mosaic obelisk that sets up its own reflections of the garden.

BELOW RIGHT Again, we have the mundane making a real contribution to the big picture, ordinary trowels as sculpture nestling among the multi-colored leaves of *Actinidia kolomikta*.

OPPOSITE These tall mirrors are purposefully set at slight angles to set up a dialogue among themselves. The background hedge provides visual stability while the carpet of coreopsis adds vibrancy and a splash of color.

Planting

Most people think that the planting of a yard or garden is a complex business, fraught with self-enforced errors that will end up with the place looking a mess. In reality, there are too many books and so-called experts who appear to go out of their way to see that this is in fact will turn out to be just the case—in short they make the thing far too complicated. This book is not one of them. Of course you can experiment and dabble endlessly with this wonderful and engrossing subject, and many people do just that, but even they will tell you that it has been a long learning curve, often acquired by a process of practical trial and error.

Planting design, and it is just that, is a part of the overall planning process, but should be entirely separate from it. In an ideal situation you should build the garden first and plant it second, you should not rush out halfway through the construction phase and bring home a car full of plants, which is more often than not a matter of succumbing to simple seduction through passing a garden center or nursery. Just step back for a moment from the perceived mystery of plants and look at the job as you would any other around the home. When you are wallpapering a room or laying a floor what is the first thing that you do? Preparation. If a surface is prepared correctly then the finished result will be perfect; if it has been prepared poorly then the resulting job will show it. It is exactly the same outside.

Soil is the medium in which plants grow and in your initial information gathering you should have checked just what it is like. A simple soil test kit, which can be bought at any garden center, will help here, telling if it is acid, alkaline or halfway in between, which in garden-speak is called neutral. If your soil is towards either end of the spectrum it will only support certain species, in other words you have acid lovers and alkaline (chalky) lovers. The soil test kit usually gives you lists of plants that enjoy each type, but if not there are plenty of books that will tell you. In addition to this your soil may be heavy clay or sandy, or simply impoverished and in need of a real boost in fertility. The other major factor with plants is sun and shade, and while some will

RIGHT The architecture and line of a garden can be greatly enhanced by planting, but the latter needs to be carefully handled and chosen to get the best out of the situation. In such a gracefully handled design the plants are kept to a sculptural minimum; remember the adage less is more. Aloes frame the water chute while the repetitive globes of cactus set up a wonderful rhythm, being underscored by dark cobbles.

RIGHT   White tulips are a celebration of a young year and this great swathe beckons you to the sitting area where you can enjoy the spring sunshine. Tulips don't naturalize as well as many bulbs so should ideally be lifted once they have died down and stored in a dry dark place until the autumn planting season.

ABOVE LEFT   Some gardens are architectural, some minimalist and some revel in the blousy embrace of plants. It would be delicious sitting here, wrapped around with a layer of flower and fragrance. Of course, such a scheme relies on a degree of maintenance but gardening is, after all, the world's most popular pastime.

ABOVE RIGHT   Containers can bring color and interest to the most uncompromising situation. Courtyards, alleys and roof gardens are often devoid of open ground and this is precisely where pots come in. Mind you, any garden room will be the richer for them, and you can change the planting on a regular basis to create an entirely new look.

grow in either, most will have a preference, and they will thrive better in one situation. Again, this is where some homework is necessary.

You will hear a lot talked about "organic" gardening and in terms of the soil preparation this means digging in as much compost and well-rotted manure as possible. Apart from being full of nutrients for the plants, this will help to make a heavy soil easier to work and bind a loose sandy soil together, giving it a better structure. Feeding soil and plants is pretty much the same as with kids: you need to keep doing it, little and often.

Now, how do you plant the spaces? Well, I often think that the people who really understand how plants associate with one another are the floral arrangers, who really have much the same eye as a good interior designer. They appreciate the importance of shape and textures of leaves: narrow against round, smooth against ribbed and so on. They also understand, particularly those that practice that most beautiful of art forms, Ikebana, that simplicity is everything, and also that flower can be a bonus, not necessarily the prime motive for choosing a plant—it is the overall shape and balance of the arrangement that is paramount. So too in your rooms outside, which are unique in so much that plants appeal to all the senses—smell, sound though the movement of wind and, of course, vision.

The difference very often between rooms inside and out is visualization. Pieces of furniture come at a predetermined size, plants don't, and they are usually small when you put them in the ground and grow over a period of years. To have a successful composition means knowing how big plants grow and in the majority of cases this, together with other information as to where the plant grows best, is on the label, so read it! In a small yard, with only limited areas to plant, it can be possible to do this on a piecemeal basis. A fragrant shade-tolerant climber against one wall. A rounded medium-height evergreen shrub with smooth leaves underplanted with a sweep of ground cover with a delicate textured foliage. A spiky plant with sword-like purple leaves, acting as a focal point, will look terrific rising above neat hummocks of silver-gray foliage, and so on. In truth the names of plants are almost immaterial at this stage, it's the characteristics of the things that are so important. Work the characteristics of what you want out first and select the species second—it's much easier.

This same character can also determine mood and atmosphere. Those spiky plants, or shrubs with an upright or "fastigiate" habit or particularly bold foliage are the attention-seekers; they are dramatic, upfront and upbeat, looking great in an architectural or contemporary yard. Softer, billowing plants are just the opposite, disguising a hard outline beyond, blending elements together and being altogether easier on the eye. In larger areas it can be helpful to prepare a planting plan, but again, think about the overall look of the area or border, shape, height, size, texture and then find plants that will do the job. In reality most plants only flower for a few weeks—the rest of the time the plant will need to rely on its other assets. Deciduous plants lose their leaves in winter—are they still handsome at that time with a fine structure or just a mess? Choose accordingly.

Plants in context

Something else that you should think about, particularly in a smaller, confined area, is the relationship between the plants and the boundary or divider against which they are set. In a large space there may well be room for an ample depth of planting where you can contrast all those different heights, textures and colors, but this will not be possible where space is limited. Let's say you have a terracotta-washed wall: Just what would you place against it? Well, in this kind of situation an architectural outline will be superb—the structure of *Nandina domestica* (heavenly bamboo) with its delicate

TOP LEFT Agaves, succulents and the like are the hard men of a garden and do well in baked-out conditions that would be the death of more tender species. It goes to prove that you should choose your plant material in relation to the climate, adding just what the particular species can bring to the situation in visual terms.

BOTTOM LEFT These are just great, little puffs of smoke leaving the top of tall chimneys. Box is one of the best town garden plants, being evergreen, tolerant of pollution and amenable to clipping in all sorts of shapes.

ABOVE To many people this is what an outside room is all about: space for a whole range of activities, easy to maintain but at the same time cocooned in planting. If you keep it simple, it works!

ABOVE RIGHT Another favorite photograph, and again just slightly laid back. The column leans a little, the old shed needs a coat of paint, but I'd leave it for a while yet, and the plants just set the thing off. Who said gardening should be hard work!

framework would look superb, underplanted with the soft round leaves of *Alchemilla mollis*. Or perhaps an imposing specimen Japanese maple with a bold sweep of bergenia below. In other words, think of what plants can add to your rooms in terms of structure and pattern and work along sound visual principles. Don't, as so often happens, plant on an ad hoc basis—the end result will almost certainly be a disjointed mess.

Color and pattern manipulates the sensation of space outside just as it does inside the house, so remember a few basic design rules. A heavily patterned wallpaper makes a room feel smaller; so do plants with big leaves. Fine feathery foliage on the other hand tends to fracture light and push a boundary away. Hot colors such as reds and yellows demand attention, drawing the eye and foreshortening space, while the cooler pastel shades engender a feeling of space and expansiveness. In a garden or outside room in which you want to increase the illusion of space keep the hotter tones close to the house or viewpoint and grade away with the cooler colors, using gray and silver as harmonizers to tie the ranges together.

At the end of the day there really isn't a great deal of difference in visual terms between plants and wallpaper, interior ornamentation and feature foliage. Some gardeners may get agitated about this, but it's all really just down to experience of putting together a look that works, both inside and out. It's fun to learn though, and it's not as complicated as you may think!

Index

Figures *in italics* indicate captions.

Garden designers and suppliers whose work features in this book

David Stevens
Well House
60 Well Street
Buckingham
Buckinghamshire MK18 1EN
+44 (0)1280 821097
gardens@david-stevens.co.uk
www.david-stevens.co.uk

National and international garden design, garden design correspondence course

Luciano Giubbilei Design
Studio E6
71 Warriner Gardens
London SW11 4XW
+44 (0)20 7622 2616
www.lucianogiubbilei.com
garden@lucianogiubbilei.com

Phillip Osman Garden Designs
48 Ferndale Road
Gorse Hill
Swindon SN2 1EX
+44 (0)1793 522498
www.phillposman.com
info@phillposman.com

Kristof Swinnen
Ankerstraat 29
9100 Sint-Niklaas
Belgium
0032 3 7101151
0032 476 328596
Fax: 0032 3 7714856
info@swinnenkristof.com
www.swinnenkristof.com
Coral Browning Gardens
21479 Encina Road

Topanga
California 90290
001 (310) 455-8910
Coralgardens@earthlink.net

The Garden Escape Ltd
Up Beyond
Wye View Lane
Symonds Yat West
Herefordshire
HR9 6B
+44 (0)870 242 7024
www.thegardenescape.co.uk
E: info@thegardenescape.co.uk

Hut Design
Unit 8B
Canford Business Park
Magna Road Wimborne
Dorset BH21 3BT
+44 (0)1202 574 584
www.hutdesign.co.uk
info@hutdesign.co.uk

Author's acknowledgements

Writing books is both hard work and fun, but would be impossible without the team, and we are a real team, that helps to put everything together.

This is my second book for Jacqui Small and her great team who have the ultimate responsibility for making things work; it's always a pleasure to collaborate with you Jacqui and the sandwiches are great.

My editor, Sian Parkhouse who is an absolute professional and all round terrific person. Simon Daley, the designer, whose skill in layout is absolutely vital in a book that focuses on creating the best outside rooms and Emily Hedges who had the gargantuan task of assembling the hundreds of photographs that are needed to put the publication together.

One more person was key to success, my old friend Jerry Harpur who labored tirelessly over the photography. I know this was a tough one Jerry and I sincerely thank you.

Picture credits

The publishers would like to thanks the following sources for their kind permission to reproduce the photographs and illustrations in this book.

Front endpaper JH/Des: Phillip Osman, RHS Hampton Court 2006, 1 Jacqui Small/Andrew Wood/A house in Marrakech, designed by Karl Fournier and Olivier Marty, Studio KO, 2 Jacqui Small/Andrew Wood/A house near Grasse, France, designed by Collett-Zarzycki Architects & Designers, 4L Garden Picture Library/Gary Rogers, 4C JH/Des: Peter Nixon, Sydney, NSW, Australia, 4R JH/Des: Phoebe Pape, NSW, Australia, 5L Jacqui Small/Andrew Wood, 5C JH/Des: Jorn Langberg, Suffolk, 5R Jacqui Small/Simon Upton/Mr & Mrs Sagbakken's cabin in Norway, 6-7 MH/Des: Leeds Metropolitan University, RHS Chelsea 2006, 8-9 JH/Des: Christopher Masson, London, 11TL JH/Chaumant Festival, France, 11TC JH/Des: Sir Terence Conran, RHS Chelsea 2004, 11TR JH/Simon & Amanda Mehigan, Old Rectory, Netherbury, 11LC JH/Des: Mark Rios, Los Angeles, Ca, 11C Jacqui Small/Andrew Wood/Abraham & Thakore, 11RC & 11BL JH/Des: Vladimir Djurovic, Lebanon, 11BC JH/Titoki Point, New Zealand, 11BR JH/Des: Topher Delaney, San Francisco, Ca, 13 Jaqcui Small/Andrew Wood/a house in East Hampton, US, designed by Selldorf Architects,14 Andreas von Einsiedel, architecture by Collett Zarzycki, 15 JH/Larry and Stephanie Feeny, Bellinghahm, Wa,16T Jacqui Small/Simon Upton/A farmouse near Toulouse designed by Kathryn Ireland, 16B JH/Des: Donald Walsh, NYC, 17 Jacqui Small/Andrew Wood/Abraham & Thakore, 18-19 JH/ Des: Vladimir Djurovic for Jimmy Bassil, Lebanon, 20 JH/Des: Ulf Nordfjell, Stockholm, 21 JH/Des: Jonathan Baillie, 22L JH/Simon & Amanda Mehigan, Old Rectory, Netherbury, 22R Jacqui Small/Frederic Vasseur/Rachel Parnaby's home in London, 23 JH/Des: Juan Grimm, Santiago, Chile, 24-27 JH/Des: Luciano Giubbilei, London, 29 JH/Des: Chris Rosmini, California, 30 JH/Cali Doxiadis, Corfu, Greece, 31 JH/ Des: Topher Delaney, San Francisco, Ca, 32-33 JH/Des: Sir Terence Conran, RHS Chelsea 2004, 33R Jacqui Small/Simon Upton/Architect Gilles Pellerin's house in Cannes, 34-37 JH/Des: Steve Martino, Phoenix, Ar, 38-41 JH/Phillip Osman, RHS Hampton Court 2006, 42-44 JH/Des: Jenny Jones,

Highwater Designs, 47 JH/Des: Bunny Guinness, RHS Chelsea 1995, 48L MH/Judith Sharpe, RHS Chelsea 2001, 48R JH/Chaumant Festival, France, 49T JH/Des: Simon Fraser, Chiswick, London, 49B JH/Bonython Manor, Helston, Cornwall, 50L JH/Chaumant Festival, France, 50TR JH/Des: Justin Greer, London, 50BR JH/Des: Topher Delaney for San Diego Children's Hospital, Ca, 51 JH/Des: Topher Delaney, 52 JH/Des: Vladamir Djurovic, Beirut, Lebanon, 53L JH/Des: Garrett Ekbo, California, 53R JH/Des: Buckman & Peterson, 54-55 JH/Des: Mark Rios, Los Angeles, Ca, 56-59 JH/Des: Coral Browning, 61 JH/Des: Mark Gregory, RHS Chelsea, 62 JH/Des: Matthew Unwin, RHS Hampton Court 2006, 63T The Garden Escape, 63B Johnathan Satchell/ www.hutdesign.co.uk, 64 JH/Alistair Davidson, Worcester, 65T JH/Des: Anthony Challis, RHS Hampton Court 2006, 65B JH/Titoki Point, New Zealand, 67TL JH/Des: Steve Martino, Phoenix, Ar, 67TC JH/Alistair Davidson, Worcester, 67TR JH/Des: Christopher Bradley-Hole, London, 67LC JH/Des: Kristoph Swinnen, Belgium, 67C MH/Leeds Metropolitan University, RHS Chelsea 2006, 67RC JH/Des: Vladimir Djurovic for Jimmy Bassil, 67BL JH/Kristoph Swinnen for Ingrid Coene, Belgium, 67BC JH/Des: Andrea Cochran, San Francisco, Ca, 67BR JH/David Stevens for Veronica Wardell, Bath, 69 JH/Des: Kristoph Swinnen, Belgium, 70 JH/Des: Penelope Hobhouse, 71L JH/Des: Andrea Cochran, San Francisco, Ca, 71R JH/Des: Andrea Cochran, 72BL MH/Leeds Metropolitan University, RHS Chelsea 2006, 72BR JH/Des: Peter Nixon, Sydney, NSW, Australia, 72-73T JH/Vladimir Sitta, Sydney, NSW, Australia, 74-77 JH/David Stevens for Veronica Wardell, Bath, 79 JH/Des: Dean Herald, RHS Chelsea 2006, 80T JH/Luciano Giubbilei, London, 80B JH/Des: Christopher Bradley-Hole, London, 81 JH/Marcus H Hewitt Landscapes, RHS Chelsea 2006, 82 JH/Des: Christopher Masson, London, 83 JH/Des: Arabella Lennox-Boyd, London, 84-87 JH/Kristoph Swinnen, Belgium, 88L MH/Leeds Metropolitan University, RHS Chelsea 2006, 88-89 JH/Des: Jacqueline van der Kloet, Weesp, The Netherlands, 89B JH/Des: Tom Stuart-Smith, RHS Chelsea 2006, 90 JH/Des: Jill Cowley, Park Farm, Essex, 91 JH/Des: Andy Sturgeon, RHS Chelsea 2006, 92 -94 JH/Alistair Davidson, Worcester, 96 -99 JH/Vic & Pat Griffiths, Willenhall, Staffs, 101TL & 101TC JH/Des: Christopher Bradley-Hole, RHS Chelsea Show 2004, 101TR & 101LC JH/Des: Vladimir Djurovic, Lebanon, 101C JH/ Des: Mary Reynolds, RHS Chelsea 2002, 101RC JH/ Des: Fiona Brockhoff & David Swann, Victoria, Australia, 101BL JH/Des: Roy Day and Steve Hickling, RHS Chelsea 2006, 101BC MH/Des: Jim Fogarty for Fleming Nurseries, RHS Chelsea 2004, 101BR JH/Bob Flowerdew, Norfolk, 103 JH/Des: Roly Nolen, Hyanis Port, Mass, 104 JH/Des: Roberto Burle Marx, Brazil, 105L JH/Des: William Martin, "Wigandia", Victoria, Austalia, 105R & 106 JH/Des: Steve Martino, Phoenix, Ar, 107 MH/Des: Jim Fogarty for Fleming Nurseries, RHS Chelsea, 108L JH/ Des: Jenny Jones, Highwater Designs, 108R JH/Cornerstone Garden Festival, Sonoma, Ca, 109 JH/Des: Fiona Brockhoff & David Swann, Victoria, Australia, 110 JH/Des: Luciano Giubbilei, London, 111L JH/Wollerton Old Hall, Shropshire, 111R JH/Des: Vladimir Sitta, Sydney, NSW, Australia, 112L JH/Des: Marcia Hosking, Sydney, NSW, Australia, 112R JH/Des: Steve Martino, Phoenix, Ar, 113TL JH/Des: Guy Petherman, RHS Hampton Court 2006, 113BL & 114 JH/Des: Steve Martino, Phoenix, Ar, 115 JH/Des: Christopher Bradley-Hole, RHS Chelsea 2004, 117 JH/Des: Penelope Hobhouse, 118L JH/Jardins de Prieure, Notre Dame d'Orsan, France, 118C JH/ Des: Steve Martino, Phoenix, Ar, 118R JH/Des: Ken Ruzicka, NYC, 119 JH/Pat Clarke, Harrogate,

Yorks, 120L JH/ Sam & Rita Roberts, Nantucket, 120R JH/Susan & Geoff Dyer, Toronto, 121TL JH/"Madoo" Sagaponack, NY, 121BL JH/Des: Mary Reynolds, RHS Chelsea 2002, 123 JH/Ulf Nordfjell, Stockholm, 124T JH/Des: Vladimir Djurovic, Lebanon, 124B JH/Sun House, Long Melford, 125 JH/Des: Vladimir Djurovic, Lebanon, 126L JH/Des: Jeff Mendoza, NYC, 126-127TL Clive Nichols/Joe Swift, 127BL Clive Nichols/RHS Hampton Court 1999, 129 JH/Des: Raymond Jungles, Miami, Fl, 130 JH/Helen Dillon, Dublin, 131L JH/Des: Philippa Probert, RHS Hampton Court 2006, 131R JH/Des: Fairuz Salleh, Singapore, 132TR MH/Des: Roy Day and Steve Hickling, RHS Chelsea 2006, 132BR JH/Des: David Stevens for Veronica Wardell, 133 JH/Des: Anthony Challis, RHS Hampton Court 2006, 134L JH/Des: Philip Nash for Robert van den Kerk, 134R JH/Vladimir Sitta, Sydney, NSW, Australia, 135 JH/Des: Luciano Giubbilei, London, 136 JH/Des: Christopher Masson, London, 137TL JH/Des: Sam Martin, "Exterior Architecture", London, 137BL JH/Des: Fairuz Salleh, Singapore, 138TR JH/Bob Flowerdew, Norfolk, 138L JH/Des: Michael van Valkenburg, NY, 138BR JH/Moat Cottage, Cockfield, Suffolk, 139 JH/Des: Luciano Giubbilei, London, 141 TL JH/Des: Vladimir Djurovi, Lebanon, 141 TC JH/Jamie Durie, Sydney, NSW, Australia, 141 TR JH/Des: Luciano Giubbilei, London, 141LC JH/Des: Philip Watson, Fredericksburg, Va, 141C JH/Des: Ulf Nordfjell, Stockholm, 141RC JH/Chaumant Festival, France, 141BL JH/Des: Steve Martino, Phoenix, Ar, 141BC JH/Des: Jenny Jones, Highwater Designs, 141BR JH/Sun House, Long Melford, Suffolk, 143 JH/"Nooroo", Mount Wilson, NSW, Australia, 144 Jacqui Small/Simon Upton/House in Provence designed by Jean-Louis Raynaud & Kenyon Kramer, 145L JH/Des: Richard Hartlage for Graeme Hardie, NJ, 145R MH/Barnards Farm, Essex, 146 JH/Des: Steve Martino, 147 JH/Des: Vladimir Djurovic, Lebanon, for Jimmy Bassil, 148T JH/Cilla Cooper, Aukland, NZ, 148B JH/Des: Tom Stuart-Smith, RHS Chelsea 2006, 148-149 JH/Des: Catherina Malmberg-Snodgrass, RHS Chelsea 2006, 151 JH/Nick Williams-Ellis RHS Chelsea 2006, 152 JH/Jamie Durie, Sydney, NSW, Australia, 153L JH/Helming Hall, Suffolk, 153R JH/Matthew Unwin, Landcraft, RHS Tatton Park 2006, 154T JH/Des: Richard Hartlage for Silas Mountsier, NJ, 154B JH/Des: Luciano Giubbilei, London, 155 JH/Des: Steve Martino, Phoenix, Ar, 156L&R Jacqui Small/SimonUpton/Peter & Mariijke de Wit of Domaine, 157 JH/Des: Bill Wheeler, NY, 158 JH/Des: Bradley Dyruff, Santa Barbara, Ca, 159TL JH/Des: Eric Ossart & Arnaud Mauriere, France, 159BL JH/Des: Francisco Brennand, Recife, Brazil, 160TR JH/Des: Topher Delaney, San Francisco, Ca, 160BR JH/Des: Ulf Nordfjell, Stockholm, 161 JH/Des: Charlotte Gaudette & Emmanuelle Tittley, Jardin De Metis 2002, Quebec, 162TR JH/Des: Steve Martino, Phoenix, Ar, 162B JH/Des: Phoebe Pape, NSW, Australia, 162-163 JH/Paul Martin Designs, RHS Hampton Court 2006, 164L JH/Des: Ulf Nordfjell, Stockholm, 164C JH/Elaine & John Walker, Nottinghamshire, 164R & 165 JH/Chaumant Festival, France, 167 JH/Des: Steve Martino, Phoenix, Ar, 168 JH/Ulf Nordfjell, Stockholm, 169L JH/Susan & Geoff Dyer, Toronto, 169R JH/Des: Ulf Nordfjell, Stockholm, 170T JH/Des: Steve Martino, Phoenix, Ar, 170B JH/Des: Luciano Giubbilei, London, 171L JH/Des: Simon Fraser, Chiswick, London, 171R JH/Des: Philip Watson, Fredericksburg, Va, Back endpaper JH/Des: Luciano Giubbilei, London.